California
HMH SCIENCE DIMENSIONS™
Volume 1

Grade 6
Units 1–2

Watch the cover come alive as you explore the body systems of a snail.
Download the HMH Science Dimensions AR app available on Android or iOS devices.

This Write-In Book belongs to

_____

Teacher/Room

_____

Houghton Mifflin Harcourt™

Consulting Authors

Michael A. DiSpezio

Global Educator
North Falmouth,
Massachusetts

Michael DiSpezio has authored many HMH instructional programs for Science and Mathematics. He has also authored numerous trade books and multimedia programs on various topics and hosted dozens of studio and location broadcasts for various organizations in the United States and worldwide. Most recently, he has been working with educators to provide strategies for implementing the Next Generation Science Standards, particularly the Science and Engineering Practices, Crosscutting Concepts, and the use of Evidence Notebooks. To all his projects, he brings his extensive background in science, his expertise in classroom teaching at the elementary, middle, and high school levels, and his deep experience in producing interactive and engaging instructional materials.

Marjorie Frank

Science Writer and Content-Area Reading Specialist
Brooklyn, New York

An educator and linguist by training, a writer and poet by nature, Marjorie Frank has authored and designed a generation of instructional materials in all subject areas, including past HMH Science programs. Her other credits include authoring science issues of an award-winning children's magazine, writing game-based digital assessments, developing blended learning materials for young children, and serving as instructional designer and coauthor of pioneering school-to-work software. In addition, she has served on the adjunct faculty of Hunter, Manhattan, and Brooklyn Colleges, teaching courses in science methods, literacy, and writing. For *California HMH Science Dimensions™*, she has guided the development of our K–2 strands and our approach to making connections between NGSS and Common Core ELA/literacy standards.

Acknowledgments

Cover credits: (garden snail) ©Johan Swanepoel/Alamy; (poison dart frog) ©Dirk Ercken/Alamy.

Section Header Master Art: (machinations) ©DNY59/E+/Getty Images; (rivers on top of Greenland ice sheet) ©Maria-José Viñas, NASA Earth Science News Team; (human cells, illustration) ©Sebastian Kaulitzki/Science Photo Library/Corbis; (waves) ©Alfred Pasieka/Science Source

© Houghton Mifflin Harcourt Publishing Company • Image Credits: ©HMH

Michael R. Heithaus, PhD

Dean, College of Arts, Sciences & Education
Professor, Department of Biological Sciences
Florida International University
Miami, Florida

Mike Heithaus joined the FIU Biology Department in 2003 and has served as Director of the Marine Sciences Program and Executive Director of the School of Environment, Arts, and Society, which brings together the natural and social sciences and humanities to develop solutions to today's environmental challenges. He now serves as Dean of the College of Arts, Sciences & Education. His research focuses on predator-prey interactions and the ecological importance of large marine species. He has helped to guide the development of Life Science content in *California HMH Science Dimensions™*, with a focus on strategies for teaching challenging content as well as the science and engineering practices of analyzing data and using computational thinking.

Bernadine Okoro

Access and Equity Consultant

S.T.E.M. Learning Advocate & Consultant
Washington, DC

Bernadine Okoro is a chemical engineer by training and a playwright, novelist, director, and actress by nature. Okoro went from working with patents and biotechnology to teaching in K–12 classrooms. A 12-year science educator and Albert Einstein Distinguished Fellow, Okoro was one of the original authors of the Next Generation Science Standards. As a member of the Diversity and Equity Team, her focus on Alternative Education and Community Schools and on Integrating Social-Emotional Learning and Brain-Based Learning into NGSS is the vehicle she uses as a pathway to support underserved groups from elementary school to adult education. An article and book reviewer for NSTA and other educational publishing companies, Okoro currently works as a S.T.E.M. Learning Advocate & Consultant.

Cary I. Sneider, PhD

Associate Research Professor
Portland State University
Portland, Oregon

While studying astrophysics at Harvard, Cary Sneider volunteered to teach in an Upward Bound program and discovered his real calling as a science teacher. After teaching middle and high school science in Maine, California, Costa Rica, and Micronesia, he settled for nearly three decades at Lawrence Hall of Science in Berkeley, California, where he developed skills in curriculum development and teacher education. Over his career, Cary directed more than 20 federal, state, and foundation grant projects and was a writing team leader for the Next Generation Science Standards. He has been instrumental in ensuring *California HMH Science Dimensions™* meets the high expectations of the NGSS and provides an effective three-dimensional learning experience for all students.

Program Advisors

Paul D. Asimow, PhD
Eleanor and John R. McMillan
Professor of Geology and
Geochemistry
California Institute of Technology
Pasadena, California

Joanne Bourgeois
Professor Emerita
Earth & Space Sciences
University of Washington
Seattle, WA

Dr. Eileen Cashman
Professor
Humboldt State University
Arcata, California

Elizabeth A. De Stasio, PhD
Raymond J. Herzog Professor of
Science
Lawrence University
Appleton, Wisconsin

Perry Donham, PhD
Lecturer
Boston University
Boston, Massachusetts

Shila Garg, PhD
Professor Emerita of Physics
Former Dean of Faculty & Provost
The College of Wooster
Wooster, Ohio

Tatiana A. Krivosheev, PhD
Professor of Physics
Clayton State University
Morrow, Georgia

Mark B. Moldwin, PhD
Professor of Space Sciences and
Engineering
University of Michigan
Ann Arbor, Michigan

Ross H. Nehm
Stony Brook University (SUNY)
Stony Brook, NY

Kelly Y. Neiles, PhD
Assistant Professor of Chemistry
St. Mary's College of Maryland
St. Mary's City, Maryland

John Nielsen-Gammon, PhD
Regents Professor
Department of Atmospheric
Sciences
Texas A&M University
College Station, Texas

Dr. Sten Odenwald
Astronomer
NASA Goddard Spaceflight Center
Greenbelt, Maryland

Bruce W. Schafer
Executive Director
Oregon Robotics Tournament &
Outreach Program
Beaverton, Oregon

Barry A. Van Deman
President and CEO
Museum of Life and Science
Durham, North Carolina

Kim Withers, PhD
Assistant Professor
Texas A&M University-Corpus
Christi
Corpus Christi, Texas

Adam D. Woods, PhD
Professor
California State University,
Fullerton
Fullerton, California

English Development Advisors

Mercy D. Momary
Local District Northwest
Los Angeles, California

Michelle Sullivan
Balboa Elementary
San Diego, California

Lab Safety Reviewer

Kenneth R. Roy, Ph.D.
Senior Lab Safety Compliance Consultant
National Safety Consultants, LLC
Vernon, Connecticut

Classroom Reviewers & Hands-On Activities Advisors

Julie Arreola
Sun Valley Magnet School
Sun Valley, California

Pamela Bluestein
Sycamore Canyon School
Newbury Park, California

Andrea Brown
HLPUSD Science & STEAM TOSA
Hacienda Heights, California

Stephanie Greene
Science Department Chair
Sun Valley Magnet School
Sun Valley, California

Rana Mujtaba Khan
Will Rogers High School
Van Nuys, California

Suzanne Kirkhope
Willow Elementary and Round
Meadow Elementary
Agoura Hills, California

George Kwong
Schafer Park Elementary
Hayward, California

Imelda Madrid
Bassett St. Elementary School
Lake Balboa, California

Susana Martinez O'Brien
Diocese of San Diego
San Diego, California

Craig Moss
Mt. Gleason Middle School
Sunland, California

Isabel Souto
Schafer Park Elementary
Hayward, California

Emily R.C.G. Williams
South Pasadena Middle School
South Pasadena, California

© Houghton Mifflin Harcourt Publishing Company • Image Credits: (t) ©Ryan McVay/Stone/Getty Image; (b) ©Kotangens/Adobe Stock

VOLUME 2

UNIT 3 The Flow of Energy in Systems

173

Flash floods can occur suddenly after a heavy rainfall. A lot of energy is released during a flash flood.

© Houghton Mifflin Harcourt Publishing Company • Image Credits: ©Johnny Adolphson/ Dreamstime

Foggy summer mornings in San Francisco happen as water from the Pacific Ocean evaporates into the air and then condenses. Wind carries the foggy air over land.

© Houghton Mifflin Harcourt Publishing Company • Image Credits: ©Ian Laksmana/500px/ Adobe Stock

VOLUME 3

UNIT 5 Environmental and Genetic Influence on Organisms

379

This plumage display of a male bird of paradise attracts the female. With their needs met by the rich tropical rain forest, birds of paradise can spend extra time and energy on reproduction.

A lot of plastic trash ends up in the oceans, where it affects many organisms, such as plankton, corals, fish, and whales.

Claims, Evidence, and Reasoning

Constructing an Argument

Constructing a strong argument is useful in science and engineering and in everyday life. A strong argument has three parts: a claim, evidence, and reasoning. Scientists and engineers use claims-evidence-reasoning arguments to communicate their explanations and solutions to others and to challenge or debate the conclusions of other scientists and engineers. The words *argue* and *argument* do not mean that scientists or engineers are fighting about something. Instead, this is a way to support a claim using evidence. Argumentation is a calm and rational way for people to examine all the facts and come to the best conclusion.

A **claim** is a statement that answers the question "What do you know?" A claim is a statement of your understanding of a phenomenon, answer to a question, or solution to a problem. A claim states what you think is true based on the information you have.

Evidence is any data that are related to your claim and answer the question "How do you know that?" These data may be from your own experiments and observations, reports by scientists or engineers, or other reliable data. Arguments made in science and engineering should be supported by empirical evidence. Empirical evidence is evidence that comes from observation or experiment.

Evidence used to support a claim should also be relevant and sufficient. Relevant evidence is evidence that is about the claim, and not about something else. Evidence is sufficient when there is enough evidence to fully support the claim.

Reasoning is the use of logical, analytical thought to form conclusions or inferences. Reasoning answers the question "Why does your evidence support your claim?" So, reasoning explains the relationship between your evidence and your claim. Reasoning might include a scientific law or principle that helps explain the relationship between the evidence and the claim.

© Houghton Mifflin Harcourt Publishing Company • Image Credits: ©HMH

Here is an example of a claims-evidence-reasoning argument.

Claim	Ice melts faster in the sun than it does in the shade.
Evidence	Two ice cubes of the same size were each placed in a plastic dish. One dish was placed on a wooden bench in the sun and one was placed on a different part of the same bench in the shade. The ice cube in the sun melted in 14 minutes and 32 seconds. The ice cube in the shade melted in 18 minutes and 15 seconds.
Reasoning	This experiment was designed so that the only variable that was different in the set-up of the two ice cubes was whether they were in the shade or in the sun. Because the ice cube in the sun melted almost 4 minutes faster than the one in the shade, this is sufficient evidence to say that ice melts faster in the sun than it does in the shade.

To summarize, a strong argument:

• presents a claim that is clear, logical, and well-defended
• supports the claim with empirical evidence that is sufficient and relevant
• includes reasons that make sense and are presented in a logical order

Constructing Your Own Argument

Now construct your own argument by recording a claim, evidence, and reasoning. With your teacher's permission, you can do an investigation to answer a question you have about how the world works. Or you can construct your argument based on observations you have already made about the world.

Claim	
Evidence	
Reasoning	

© Houghton Mifflin Harcourt Publishing Company

 For more information on claims, evidence, and reasoning, see the online **English Language Arts Handbook.**

Whether you are in the lab or in the field, you are responsible for your own safety and the safety of others. To fulfill these responsibilities and avoid accidents, be aware of the safety of your classmates as well as your own safety at all times. Take your lab work and fieldwork seriously, and behave appropriately. Elements of safety to keep in mind are shown below and on the following pages.

Safety in the Lab

- ☐ Be sure you understand the materials, your procedure, and the safety rules before you start an investigation in the lab.

- ☐ Know where to find and how to use fire extinguishers, eyewash stations, shower stations, and emergency power shutoffs.

- ☐ Use proper safety equipment. Always wear personal protective equipment, such as eye protection and gloves, when setting up labs, during labs, and when cleaning up.

- ☐ Do not begin until your teacher has told you to start. Follow directions.

- ☐ Keep the lab neat and uncluttered. Clean up when you are finished. Report all spills to your teacher immediately. Watch for slip/fall and trip/fall hazards.

- ☐ If you or another student is injured in any way, tell your teacher immediately, even if the injury seems minor.

- ☐ Do not take any food or drink into the lab. Never take any chemicals out of the lab.

Safety in the Field

- ☐ Be sure you understand the goal of your fieldwork and the proper way to carry out the investigation before you begin fieldwork.

- ☐ Use proper safety equipment and personal protective equipment, such as eye protection, that suits the terrain and the weather.

- ☐ Follow directions, including appropriate safety procedures as provided by your teacher.

- ☐ Do not approach or touch wild animals. Do not touch plants unless instructed by your teacher to do so. Leave natural areas as you found them.

- ☐ Stay with your group.

- ☐ Use proper accident procedures, and let your teacher know about a hazard in the environment or an accident immediately, even if the hazard or accident seems minor.

Safety Symbols

To highlight specific types of precautions, the following symbols are used throughout the lab program. Remember that no matter what safety symbols you see within each lab, all safety rules should be followed at all times.

Dress Code

- Wear safety goggles (or safety glasses as appropriate for the activity) at all times in the lab as directed. If chemicals get into your eye, flush your eyes immediately for a minimum of 15 minutes.
- Do not wear contact lenses in the lab.

- Do not look directly at the sun or any intense light source or laser.
- Wear appropriate protective non-latex gloves as directed.
- Wear an apron or lab coat at all times in the lab as directed.
- Tie back long hair, secure loose clothing, and remove loose jewelry. Remove acrylic nails when working with active flames.
- Do not wear open-toed shoes, sandals, or canvas shoes in the lab.

Glassware and Sharp Object Safety

- Do not use chipped or cracked glassware.
- Use heat-resistant glassware for heating or storing hot materials.
- Notify your teacher immediately if a piece of glass breaks.
- Use extreme care when handling any sharp or pointed instruments.
- Do not cut an object while holding the object unsupported in your hands. Place the object on a suitable cutting surface, and always cut in a direction away from your body.

Chemical Safety

- If a chemical gets on your skin, on your clothing, or in your eyes, rinse it immediately for a minimum of 15 minutes (using the shower, faucet, or eyewash station), and alert your teacher.

- Do not clean up spilled chemicals unless your teacher directs you to do so.

- Do not inhale any gas or vapor unless directed to do so by your teacher. If you are instructed to note the odor of a substance, wave the fumes toward your nose with your hand. This is called wafting. Never put your nose close to the source of the odor.
- Handle materials that emit vapors or gases in a well-ventilated area.
- Keep your hands away from your face while you are working on any activity.

Safety Symbols, continued

Electrical Safety

- Do not use equipment with frayed electrical cords or loose plugs.
- Do not use electrical equipment near water or when clothing or hands are wet.
- Hold the plug housing when you plug in or unplug equipment. Do not pull on the cord.
- Use only GFI-protected electrical receptacles.

Heating and Fire Safety

- Be aware of any source of flames, sparks, or heat (such as flames, heating coils, or hot plates) before working with any flammable substances.
- Know the location of the lab's fire extinguisher and fire-safety blankets.
- Know your school's fire-evacuation routes.
- If your clothing catches on fire, walk to the lab shower to put out the fire. Do not run.
- Never leave a hot plate unattended while it is turned on or while it is cooling.
- Use tongs or appropriately insulated holders when handling heated objects.
- Allow all equipment to cool before storing it.

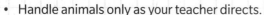

Plant and Animal Safety

- Do not eat any part of a plant.
- Do not pick any wild plant unless your teacher instructs you to do so.
- Handle animals only as your teacher directs.
- Treat animals carefully and respectfully.
- Wash your hands thoroughly with soap and water after handling any plant or animal.

Cleanup

- Clean all work surfaces and protective equipment as directed by your teacher.
- Dispose of hazardous materials or sharp objects only as directed by your teacher.
- Wash your hands thoroughly with soap and water before you leave the lab or after any activity.

Student Safety Quiz

Circle the letter of the BEST answer.

1. Before starting an investigation or lab procedure, you should
   A. try an experiment of your own
   B. open all containers and packages
   C. read all directions and make sure you understand them
   D. handle all the equipment to become familiar with it

2. At the end of any activity you should
   A. wash your hands thoroughly with soap and water before leaving the lab
   B. cover your face with your hands
   C. put on your safety goggles
   D. leave hot plates switched on

3. If you get hurt or injured in any way, you should
   A. tell your teacher immediately
   B. find bandages or a first aid kit
   C. go to your principal's office
   D. get help after you finish the lab

4. If your glassware is chipped or broken, you should
   A. use it only for solid materials
   B. give it to your teacher for recycling or disposal
   C. put it back into the storage cabinet
   D. increase the damage so that it is obvious

5. If you have unused chemicals after finishing a procedure, you should
   A. pour them down a sink or drain
   B. mix them all together in a bucket
   C. put them back into their original containers
   D. dispose of them as directed by your teacher

6. If electrical equipment has a frayed cord, you should
   A. unplug the equipment by pulling the cord
   B. let the cord hang over the side of a counter or table
   C. tell your teacher about the problem immediately
   D. wrap tape around the cord to repair it

7. If you need to determine the odor of a chemical or a solution, you should
   A. use your hand to bring fumes from the container to your nose
   B. bring the container under your nose and inhale deeply
   C. tell your teacher immediately
   D. use odor-sensing equipment

8. When working with materials that might fly into the air and hurt someone's eye, you should wear
   A. goggles
   B. an apron
   C. gloves
   D. a hat

9. Before doing experiments involving a heat source, you should know the location of the
   A. door
   B. window
   C. fire extinguisher
   D. overhead lights

10. If you get chemicals in your eye you should
    A. wash your hands immediately
    B. put the lid back on the chemical container
    C. wait to see if your eye becomes irritated
    D. use the eyewash station right away, for a minimum of 15 minutes

Go online to view the Lab Safety Handbook for additional information.

Science and Engineering

How do humans explore and design our world?

This rocket car was developed and engineered for optimized speed. Each year people gather in Black Rock Desert, Nevada, to watch cars similar to this break the world land-speed record.

You Solve It How Can You Plan Efficient Cargo Shipping? Design an efficient way to deliver cars to two different ports by choosing the sizes of your ships, their shipping routes, and the size of your shipments.

Go online and complete the You Solve It to explore ways to solve a real-world problem.

Optimize a Race Track

This wooden track is designed to keep the model race cars moving in a straight line.

A. Look at the photo. On a separate sheet of paper, write down as many different questions as you can about the photo.

B. **Discuss** With your class or a partner, share your questions. Record any additional questions generated in your discussion. Then choose the most important questions from the list that are related to designing, testing, and improving a track design. Write them below.

C. Choose a feature of the track you can test to see if and how it influences the speed of cars that use the track. Remember, in any iteration of the track, the finish line needs to be lower than the starting point, as the cars depend on the force of gravity to move them. What design feature of the track, or variable, will you investigate?

D. Use the information above, and your research, to develop a solution that will improve the speed of cars on the track.

👉 *Discuss the next steps for your Unit Project with your teacher and go online to download the Unit Project Worksheet.*

Language Development

Use the lessons in this unit to complete the network and expand your understanding of these key concepts.

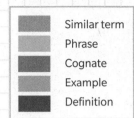

Similar term
Phrase
Cognate
Example
Definition

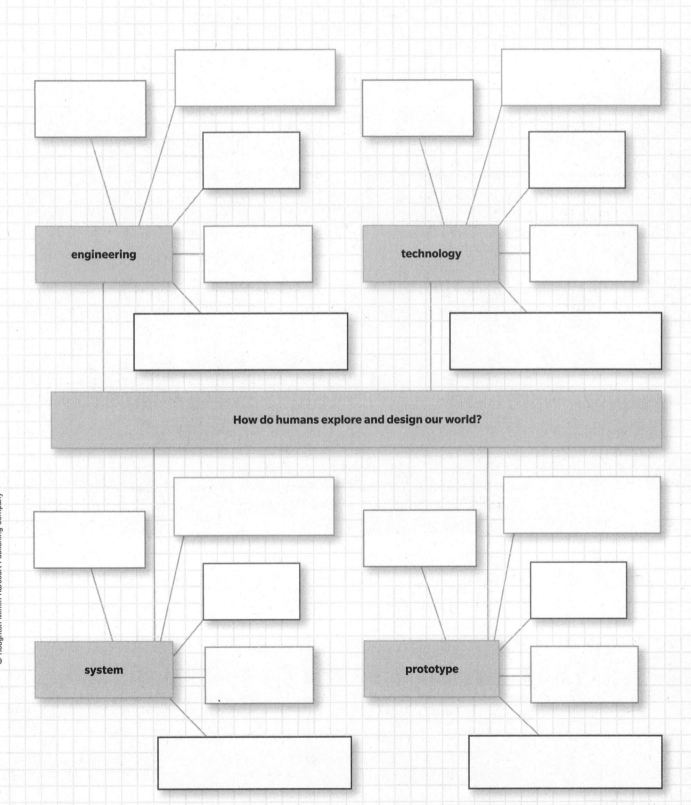

engineering

technology

How do humans explore and design our world?

system

prototype

Engineering, Science, and Society Are Related

Precisely cut and fitted dry stone walls are characteristic of Incan architecture. The wall design made structures, such as this one in Machu Picchu in Peru, earthquake resistant.

Explore First

Comparing Wall Structures Model several rectangular bricks out of modeling clay. Construct a small wall using half of the bricks. Sculpt the remaining bricks so they fit in a similar way to the carved, fitted stones shown in the photo. Then, construct a wall with these bricks. How can you test the stability of each wall? Which one is more stable?

CAN YOU EXPLAIN IT?

What needs influenced the development of mosquito netting?

Insecticide-treated mosquito nets help prevent the spread of malaria in developing countries. Malaria is spread by mosquito bites. The nets must meet the needs of the people who use them.

1. Does the solution to an engineering problem have to address every need of its users? Explain your answer.

2. Does a successful engineered solution to a problem have to be electronic? Explain your answer.

EVIDENCE NOTEBOOK As you explore the lesson, gather evidence to explain the needs that would influence the development of mosquito netting.

Relating Science, Engineering, and Technology

Science is the study of phenomena. It is a search for explanations of events, processes, or objects based on logic and evidence. Scientific discoveries help explain systems and phenomena. Engineering is related to science. **Engineering** is the systematic practice of solving problems with designed solutions. Solutions designed and built by engineers are examples of technology. **Technology** is any tool, process, or system that is designed to solve a problem. The designed world includes all parts of the environment that were made by people. You are surrounded by the designed world. You depend on it. The designed world exists within the natural world.

Explore Online

A volcanologist walks near the vent of an active volcano. Lava can range in temperature from 700 °C–1,250 °C (approximately 1,200 °F–2,200 °F).

3. **Discuss** Together with a partner, review the photo above. This scientist is using several engineered items to carry out his or her research. What are some of the items, and what might their purpose be?

Scientists Use Engineered Tools to Explore the Natural World

Scientific discoveries help increase our understanding of the world around us. Scientists often rely on engineered tools, such as computers and measuring devices, to carry out research. These tools "extend" our senses and abilities. They allow us to sense and process events that would otherwise be invisible to us. For example, telescopes allow us to study phenomena that are too far away for human eyes to see. Computers quickly carry out calculations that would take a human brain much longer to do.

Many phenomena are difficult to observe directly. Engineers may design materials and systems to aid scientific study. For example, special clothing, vehicles, and breathing devices allow scientists to stay underwater to study aquatic life. Satellites collect images and other data from great heights above Earth's surface. Microscopes visualize objects that are too small for the human eye to see. Advances in engineering such as these have greatly changed scientific exploration.

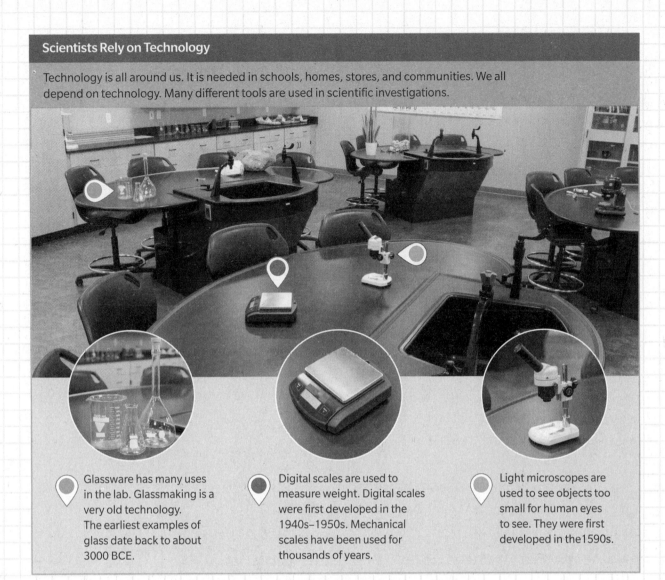

Scientists Rely on Technology

Technology is all around us. It is needed in schools, homes, stores, and communities. We all depend on technology. Many different tools are used in scientific investigations.

Glassware has many uses in the lab. Glassmaking is a very old technology. The earliest examples of glass date back to about 3000 BCE.

Digital scales are used to measure weight. Digital scales were first developed in the 1940s–1950s. Mechanical scales have been used for thousands of years.

Light microscopes are used to see objects too small for human eyes to see. They were first developed in the1590s.

4. What are the basic scientific principles the engineers who designed the digital scales would have needed to understand to design this tool? Choose all that apply.

   A. electric currents

   B. physical properties of metals

   C. influence of gravitational force on objects

   D. physical and chemical properties of materials used in building circuits

5. Identify two tools in the lab classroom: one that is used to measure volume and another that is used to observe objects. How would not having those tools affect your ability to carry out lab assignments?

Engineers Rely on Science

To build cars, engineers must have a strong understanding of science and math principles that relate to cars, such as:

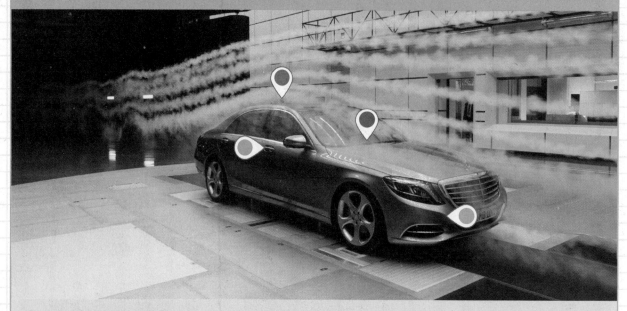

 human anatomy and physiology, to design safe and comfortable interiors and exteriors.

forces and energy, to understand the effects of gravity, friction, and collision forces on cars and the materials of which they are made.

aerodynamics, including thrust and drag, to design sleek and efficient car bodies.

 energy transmission by waves, for functioning of radio, interactive screens, and wireless software.

Engineers Use Science to Solve Practical Problems

Before a solution can be developed, the problem itself must be accurately defined. This can be done by identifying precisely what the solution needs to do. For example, the request that a car horn be "loud" is not precise. "Loud" is not a measurable value. However, "a car horn that is 95 decibels" is a more precise design description that will help engineers develop a better product.

Imagine a team of engineers working to design a new car for a car manufacturer. The car has to meet certain safety requirements and the needs of the market, and not be too expensive to manufacture. Consumer safety laws require car makers to build safe cars for their customers. The engineers might like to build a car that can reach high speeds, and customers might like that too. However, if the design of a car makes it dangerous, the car would have difficulty meeting safety laws.

In order to evaluate different car designs and materials, the design team needs to apply knowledge of many scientific principles. Qualities such as the physical properties, chemical properties, and the strength of materials are tested. In this way, engineers depend on science to develop new technologies. Discoveries made by scientists can also inspire engineers. For example, carbon fiber was discovered by a scientist studying the physical properties of carbon. Carbon fiber is made from long strands of carbon atoms that are woven together. It is light, strong, and resists high temperatures. These properties made carbon fiber suitable for use in cars and car parts.

© Houghton Mifflin Harcourt Publishing Company • Image Credits: ©Franziska Kraufmann/dpa/Corbis

6. Use the word bank to complete the table below by identifying the type of design concern that each question addresses. Some of the questions may address more than one engineering concern.

- resource availability
- ~~environmental concerns~~
- safety concerns
- production costs
- consumer demands

Question	Type of Design Concern
How can chemical pollutants emitted by the car be minimized?	environmental concerns
How can the supply of steel and other raw materials be obtained for the best price?	
How do different parts of the car withstand collisions?	
How can reliable wireless connectivity be added to the car design?	

Solve a Food Storage Problem

The modern canning process was developed in the early 19th century as a safe way to preserve, store, and transport food while minimizing spoilage. Canning was originally developed to feed an army, but it was quickly adapted for nonmilitary purposes. A preservation method that minimized the number of harmful microbes in the food, kept it relatively tasty, and made it easy to store and transport was a need society had too, and canned food was an answer. Canned foods remain fresh for much longer than fresh foods. Before refrigeration was common, canned foods were in great demand as a way of keeping food at home. Modern canning is made possible by applying knowledge of many sciences, including biology, chemistry, and physics, to a real-life problem. Cans also created the need for another engineered object: the can opener!

Canning technology has many parts.

① Sealing the cans to make them air tight.

② Making the cans tough enough to withstand knocks and bumps.

③ Heating the foods to high enough temperatures to kill harmful microbes.

④ Ensuring that material from the can doesn't dissolve into the food.

⑤ Designing the lids and bottoms of the cans so they are easy to stack.

7. Many modern can designs include a ring pull that allows the lid to be pulled off by hand instead of cut off with a can opener. What need might have led to such a design change?

_____

_____

_____

_____

_____

_____

Analyzing Systems and Models

Scientists and engineers work with systems. A **system** is a set of parts, or *components*, that interact. A video game system includes game controls with computer graphics and sound. Your immune system helps your body fight disease. Some systems are natural. Other systems are engineered, or designed by people. Scientists study natural and designed systems to understand how they function, while engineers design or improve systems to solve problems. The lock and dam shown below is a system that engineers designed to help boats travel up and down rivers with large slopes.

The Parts of a System

Systems are made up of parts, or *components*. They may be made up of smaller *subsystems*, such as the movable dam gates in the example below. The gate subsystem is made up of strong metal doors and the motors that move them. Systems also have *inputs*, *processes*, and *outputs*. Boats are one of the inputs to the lock and dam system. They move into it, then move out of it at a different level. Systems also have *boundaries*. The boundaries of the lock and dam system are the gates that separate it from the river.

A Simplified Lock and Dam System

This engineered system has solved transportation problems for hundreds of years.

Explore Online

direction of current

direction of boat

A boat enters the lock system when the gate is open. Once the gate is closed behind the vessel, water is pumped into the lock through the filling valve. This causes the water level in the lock to rise.

Filling valves also release water from a lock to lower the water level. Lowering the water level in the lock allows the vessel to move smoothly downstream.

When a vessel is moving upstream, water is added to the lock by the filling valve to equal the upstream water level. This allows the vessel to travel upstream against the direction of the current.

8. Fill in the blanks to best complete the following statements.

The lock and dam together form a(n) _____ with _____ at the higher and lower river levels. Water moving through the lock starts as a(n) _____ and ends as a(n) _____.

WORD BANK
- system
- boundaries
- output
- input

System Models

Systems and their interactions can be very complex. Scientists and engineers often rely on models and simulations to better understand and predict the behavior of systems. A scientific model shows the structure of an object, system, or concept. Simulations use models to imitate the function, behavior, or process under different conditions.

Engineers use system models to explore how a designed system works. They may also discover what might be going wrong in a system. Investigating a system model is usually safer, less expensive, and easier than carrying out investigations on the real-world system. For example, carrying out earthquake tests on scaled-down building models is much cheaper, easier, and safer than carrying out tests on a full-scale building. Testing scale models like this can help identify potential problems with structural designs or materials.

Two scale models of buildings are tested on a shake table. One of the models is of an earthquake resistant design.

9. Do the Math Though models and simulations have many benefits, some factors or conditions must be approximated. Others cannot be reasonably included at all.

Imagine you are an engineer who needs to test a scale model of a footbridge. It will be a $\frac{1}{20}$ scale model. The footbridge will cross over a busy road and allow people to cross the road safely. How could a relatively small design error of 2 centimeters in the model system cause a significant problem in construction of the bridge?

Different Models Meet Different Needs

Different types of models allow scientists and engineers to test ideas and find solutions to difficult problems. A physical model represents the physical structure of an object or system. Physical models often look and work like the object or system they represent. Mathematical models are made up of numbers and equations. These models can often be shown as graphs and may be used to predict future trends. A conceptual or mental model is a way of thinking about how parts of a system are related in order to simplify complex relationships. Some computer models are like physical models in that they show the physical structure of an object. Other computer models are more like mathematical models.

The proportions, scale, and quantities used in a model must reflect the real-life object or system. For example, in modeling the piers and beams of a bridge, the scaled-down models must have the same proportions as the full-scale bridge. If not, the data collected while testing the model will not be valid. Models are also useful to run scenarios that would be impossible to test in real life, such as what may happen if Earth's temperature increased by 10 °C.

EVIDENCE NOTEBOOK

10. Keeping mosquitoes away from people is one of the needs mosquito netting should address. What type(s) of models might be useful in testing a solution to that need? Record your evidence.

Evaluate Benefits of Crash Testing

Seat belts and airbags are two technologies that have been demonstrated to be effective in crash simulations. These simulations, or crash tests, use physical, full-size models of cars, drivers, and passengers. They are very expensive to conduct, so a lot of data is gathered during these tests to make them worthwhile. Automotive crash tests and the data collected from them have led to stricter safety guidelines for car manufacturers. This has reduced injuries in car accidents over time.

Explore Online

11. What are the benefits of crash tests? Select all that apply.

   A. They do not put people in danger.

   B. They allow engineers to test new designs.

   C. The type and speed of the crash can be controlled.

   D. There is very little cost in performing the test.

12. What solutions would you propose to a car manufacturer if its car rated poorly in a crash test?

_____

_____

_____

Analyzing Influences on Technology

Technology helps people to meet needs such as food, shelter, and clothing. The ways we communicate, play, and move from place to place are also shaped by technology. The bicycle is an example of a technology that has changed over time, for several reasons. Many bike design changes resulted from safety concerns, ease of use, or society's demands and needs. For example, societal changes such as the increasing independence of women led to the development of "safety bicycles." These bikes were designed to be safer and easier to ride than the large-wheeled penny farthings. The increased popularity of safety bikes caused a "bicycle craze" in the 1890s.

Influences on Bike Design

Today's bicycles are products of many changes over time. Each design change solved a problem that was present in previous designs.

1817

The earliest bicycles, such as the draisine, were made of wood and did not have pedals, brakes, a chain, or adjustable seats. They were designed to be propelled by the user pushing his or her feet off the ground.

1890s

Safety concerns about the awkward penny farthing led to the development of safety bicycles. These bikes had chains, gears, brakes, and air-filled tires, which allowed for easier steering and pedaling and increased comfort.

1960s–1970s

Increasing interest in exercise influenced the design of road bikes, BMX roadsters, mountain bikes, and commuter bikes.

1870s

The penny farthing had a large front wheel and a tiny rear wheel. They moved when the rider pushed on pedals that were attached directly to the large front wheel. The seat of the bike was quite high off the ground. The bike did not have brakes. It was difficult to steer and pedal, and remaining balanced was difficult. Cyclists often fell off and got hurt.

Today

Materials technology has advanced so much that some bicycles are made of wood and bamboo— a return to materials the earliest bikes were made of!

13. In 1887, a Scottish vet named John Boyd Dunlop designed an air-filled bike tire after his son had difficulty learning to ride a tricycle with hard rubber tires. This is an example of a technology being inspired by a(n) _societal / individual_ need.

Scientific Understanding Influences Technology

Scientific discoveries result in new kinds of technology. One modern example of this can be seen in the development of computer technology. Computing advanced rapidly in the 20th century. These advances were due to improved scientific understanding of such things as electric circuits and the physical properties of materials called semiconductors. The components used to control the flow of electric current in computers are now much smaller and more efficient than the large components used in the earliest computers. Over time, computers became smaller, faster, and more efficient because their components were made smaller, faster, and more efficient. Today's computers process data more rapidly and are able to share data more easily than earlier computers.

The earliest computers, such as this UNIVAC 1103, were very large and expensive. They were often the size of a room. They were mostly used by the government and military to perform complex calculations from large amounts of data.

Modern computers are thousands of times faster and have far more memory than the earliest household computers. Although the Internet was originally developed for scientists, people now use it for everyday activities.

14. List one positive influence and one negative influence that computers have on society.

15. Write What would happen if every piece of technology around you were to disappear?

The Environment Influences Technology

The environment has influenced the development of technologies for thousands of years. For example, archaeologists found evidence that early farmers developed ways to capture rainwater to irrigate their crops. People living in cold climates drove the development of heating technologies, while people living in hot climates drove the development of air conditioning. The presence of fast-flowing rivers led to the development of hydroelectric power. The understanding that burning fossil fuels is changing climates has led to the development of wind turbines and solar cells, which help generate electrical energy without the use of fossil fuels.

© Houghton Mifflin Harcourt Publishing Company • Image Credits: (l) ©NASA; (r) ©sot/Photodisc/Getty Images

Society Influences Technology

Technology is everywhere. Technology is an important part of modern life. Humans have been engineering solutions to practical problems for a long time. The earliest forms of technology, such as lighting fire, spears, cutting tools, and clothing, helped people gather food efficiently and stay warm. The basic needs for food, shelter, safety, and warmth influenced the development of many technologies, and still do today.

Some modern technologies, such as snack foods, continue to be developed due to consumer interests or wants rather than needs. Consumer demand for watching movies on their phones has led to the design of phones with larger screens and the development of faster online streaming services. Many other technologies have been developed in response to changing attitudes and cultural norms.

For example, social awareness of the needs of people with physical disabilities has increased over time. Current laws require that schools, public transport, and living spaces be accessible to people who use wheelchairs and other assistive devices. Such requirements have led to the development of different assistive technologies such as chairlifts, showering benches, and assistive listening devices.

Laws that affect the mining and processing of materials can influence technology. Environmental laws such as the U.S. Clean Air Act and the Clean Water Act limit the amount of pollution that can be produced during manufacturing processes. Safety and health laws limit employees' exposure to hazardous conditions that could happen during mining or manufacturing processes.

16. In the 1970s, the U.S. Environmental Protection Agency put limits on vehicle emissions because pollution from vehicle exhausts was linked to human diseases. As a result, car makers had to develop technologies that reduced pollutants in vehicle exhausts. What limit to technology does this situation represent? Choose all that apply.

   A. a social change that resulted in a natural change

   B. a new technology that was informed by a scientific finding

   C. a change in the law that resulted in society limiting technology

   D. a technological change that resulted in a scientific discovery

Consumer demand for more interactive entertainment has influenced the size of TV screens and the development of smart TV technology.

Unvented gas space heaters were once commonly built into new homes. They have been banned in most U.S. states due to the risk of carbon monoxide poisoning.

Indoor bathrooms were once a luxury. Before the early 20th century, homes did not usually have toilets. People used outdoor toilets in small sheds called outhouses.

EVIDENCE NOTEBOOK

17. Mosquitoes that spread diseases such as malaria are more common in climates that are very warm. How would the climate of an area affect the design of a mosquito net to be used there? Record your evidence.

Language SmArts

Identify Influences on Technology

Transportation is a vital part of modern life. But meeting the transportation needs of a community can be difficult. Extreme landscapes, rough terrain, and the need to preserve sensitive ecosystems all add to that challenge. Bridges, railways, and roads are transportation systems that require careful engineering. These technologies must meet complex environmental, physical, and societal needs, from minimizing the impact on the environment to maximizing the safety for users of the roadways. Civil engineers who design roadways consider factors such as material availability, motorist safety, and the effects of the structures and road system on wildlife.

The invention of different technologies influenced the design of roadways over time. Bicycles, asphalt, concrete, steel, cars, expanding business markets, and laws have all influenced the design of roads in different ways.

Dirt roads once connected many American cities. These paths, originally designed for traveling on foot, by horse, or by stagecoach, were simple to make and maintain, but could quickly become uneven, muddy, or dangerous.

Highways allow billions of vehicles to travel across great distances. Modern highway systems are also impressive feats of civil engineering. The U.S. highway system was one of the largest engineering projects ever built in the country.

18. Many factors have driven the development of roadway technology throughout history. What factor do you think likely had the greatest influence? Would you describe it as a social, scientific, or environmental factor? Use what you have read in this lesson to support your claim.

_____

_____

_____

_____

_____

_____

© Houghton Mifflin Harcourt Publishing Company • Image Credits: (l) Library of Congress, LC-USZ62-29715; (r) Digital Vision/Getty Images RF

Assessing the Impact of Technology on Society

Technology and Society Affect Each Other

The development of a technology does not guarantee its widespread use. A community's values and environmental conditions play a role in determining which technologies are developed and used. As shown below, identifying the effect of technology on society calls for an understanding of social and environmental factors.

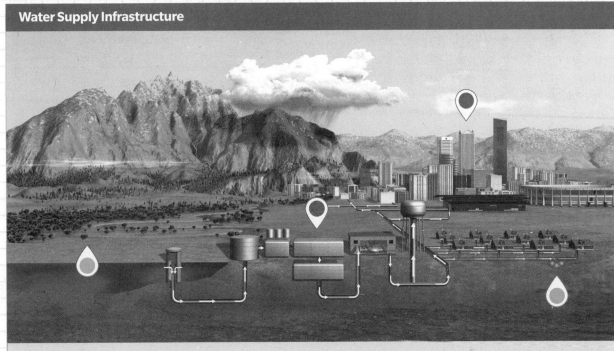

Water Supply Infrastructure

Processes for supplying water to a community can differ depending on the abundance and quality of water in the region.

People in a community may have different expectations of the water supplied to their homes. Is it safe? Is it free of harmful organisms? Does it contain harmful substances? These expectations may change over time, or vary from person to person.

Towns and cities in dry or hot climates may have higher water needs than towns and cities in wet, rainy climates. For example, in dry climates, more water may be needed for growing crops and gardens.

The cost of repairing or replacing an existing water supply network is an important factor in maintaining access to clean water for residents. A technology is not useful to a community that cannot afford to purchase, maintain, or repair it.

19. How does climate most likely affect the water distribution system?

   A. If the area has a dry climate, water resources are likely to be limited or need to be pumped from farther away.

   B. If the area has a dry climate, people will need less water.

   C. If the area has a dry climate, the community cannot afford to replace cracked or rusted pipes.

   D. If the area has a dry climate, people in the community are more concerned about contamination of the water supply.

Technology Can Improve Quality of Life

Technology helps people accomplish everyday tasks. Technology allows people to travel by land, air, and sea, and to communicate with others all over the world. Medical technology has made many diseases easier to control or even cure. For example, controlling diabetes with medicine was once thought to be impossible, and organ transplants were experimental technologies. Today, both types of treatments are commonplace.

Assistive and adaptive technology plays a very important role in helping people in their daily lives. This type of technology includes devices such as hearing aids, wheelchairs, and titanium rods used to set broken bones. Other examples include devices that replace damaged or lost limbs, help keep hearts beating with a regular rhythm, and focus blurry vision.

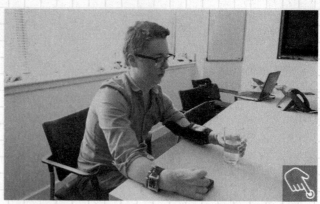

Some prosthetics have electrodes that connect to a person's nerves. These devices are controlled by the user's brain.

20. Identify the human needs that are addressed by the technologies listed in the table.

Technology	Issue to be addressed
hearing aid	
wheelchair	
glasses	
medicine	

21. Name two benefits that a modern electronic prosthetic device might have over an older, nonelectronic one.

EVIDENCE NOTEBOOK

22. Mosquito netting is most commonly used in developing countries. It is relatively cheap to make and is often distributed for free. What societal needs would demand that a tool be inexpensive to make or to buy? Record your evidence.

Hands-On Lab
Investigate a Technology Inspired by Nature

Investigate a design problem that was solved with a nature-inspired solution, and identify a need that could also be met by a nature-inspired solution.

Biomimicry is the design and use of tools or solutions that copy natural structures or processes. For example, in 1941, a Swiss engineer named George de Mestral noticed that burs got stuck in his dog's fur and in his own clothes. De Mestral was very curious about what made them so "sticky." He viewed the burs under a microscope. What he saw inspired him to invent a hook-and-loop fastener he called Velcro®. In this investigation, you will observe the structure of burs to see how it influences their function and how they inspired such a useful tool.

Cockleburs produce a fruit called a bur, which contains seeds. Burs are covered in tiny hooks that attach to animals' fur, which helps disperse the seeds.

Procedure

STEP 1 Obtain a bur and square of fun fur. Take turns observing how the bur sticks to the fun fur.

STEP 2 Observe the bur and the fur, using the magnifying lens. Describe their structure in the first column of the table.

MATERIALS
- artificial animal fur (fun fur)
- cocklebur fruit (bur)
- hook-and-loop fastener
- magnifying lens

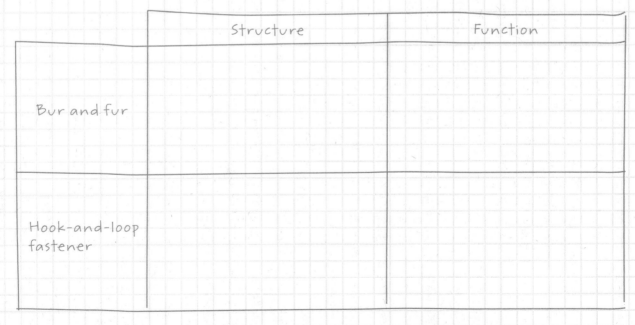

	Structure	Function
Bur and fur		
Hook-and-loop fastener		

STEP 3 In the second column of the table, describe how the bur's structure affects its function.

STEP 4 Observe the hook-and-loop fastener, using the magnifying lens the same way. In the table, describe how the hook-and-loop fastener's structure affects its function.

Identify a different need that could be solved by a nature-inspired solution.

Analysis

STEP 6 What features of your chosen object or process make it suitable to solve the problem or need you identified?

Analyze the Impact of a Technology on Society

Some types of technology have had a greater impact on society than others. Agriculture is one area in which technological advancements have had far-reaching effects. Agricultural technologies have increased the amount of food that can be grown per acre. Growing the same amount of crops but using less space means fewer existing habitats need to be cleared to make space for farmland to feed growing human populations. The areas of land that are being farmed are far more productive than they used to be. This is due to improvements in things such as plant breeding, soil preparation, harvesting, storage, and transportation.

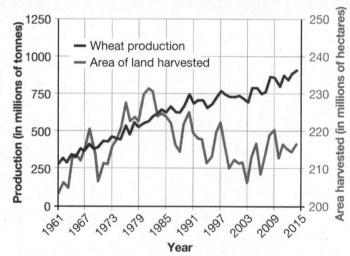

Global Wheat Production and Area of Land Harvested from 1961 to 2014

Credit: Adapted from *Global wheat production*, 1961–2014 from http://www.fao.org/faostat/en/#data/QC. Copyright © 2017 by Food and Agriculture Organization of the United Nations. Adapted and reproduced by permission of Food and Agriculture Organization of the United Nations.

23. From 1979 to 2014, the amount of wheat harvested worldwide
    decreased / increased / stayed relatively constant while the area
    of land use decreased / increased / stayed relatively constant.

24. The human population is projected to increase by 1 billion people by 2044. How will an increased demand on resources affect the need for agricultural engineering?

    _____

    _____

    _____

    _____

    _____

    _____

    _____

Continue Your Exploration

Name: _____ **Date:** _____

Check out the path below or go online to choose one of the other paths shown.

| Designing an Efficient Lunch Line | • People in Science
• Careers in Engineering
• Hands-On Labs ✋
• Propose Your Own Path | *Go online to choose one of these other paths.* |

In many situations, the solution to an engineering problem is not an object or tool but a process or a system. For example, consider a cafeteria lunch line. A school lunch line is a process that is designed to serve meals to hundreds of people in a relatively short period of time.

Examine the Needs to Be Met

This is probably a familiar sight: the school cafeteria. Have you ever thought about all the steps that go into preparing and serving school lunches every school day? The food must be transported, prepared, cooked, and served to many people. Ingredients must be monitored for freshness and nutritional content. And the meals should taste good too!

Define the Problem

Suppose that you have been challenged to improve the efficiency of your school's cafeteria. Think about the cafeteria as a system. Identify the key people, processes, and technologies that keep it running. Then, think like an engineer by asking specific questions that will help you define the design problem you will address.

Continue Your Exploration

Developing Solutions by First Asking Questions

Asking very specific questions about the problem or issue you are trying to solve will help you identify the problem. Identifying the problem precisely will help you come up with more or better solutions. Asking questions will also help you identify the important and nonimportant factors of the problem. For example, asking, "How many people use the cafeteria each day?", "What are the most popular meals and foods the cafeteria serves?", or "How long is the average wait for food on the busiest day?" will help you pinpoint possible problems that you can work toward solving.

1. What needs are not being met by a slow-moving or busy line at a school cafeteria?

2. Identify the people, processes, and technologies that play a role in the issue you identified. Now, identify a factor that is *unlikely* to influence the length of time people wait in the lunch line.

3. Identify one change in the cafeteria process that might make the lunch line more efficient.

4. **Collaborate** Serving fresh, nutritious food to several hundred people every day in a cafeteria is a design challenge. How might nutrition science and engineering affect each other?

Can You Explain It?

Name: _____   **Date:** _____

What needs influenced the development of mosquito netting?

EVIDENCE NOTEBOOK

Refer to your notes in your Evidence Notebook to help you construct an explanation of the needs that influenced development of mosquito netting.

1. State your claim. Make sure your claim fully explains how the needs you mention are related to the development of mosquito netting as a solution to the spread of disease.

2. Summarize the evidence you have gathered to support your claim and explain your reasoning.

Checkpoints

Answer the following questions to check your understanding of the lesson.

Use the photo to answer Questions 3 and 4.

3. What need is addressed by the simple technology the girl in the photo is using?

    A. keeping hair untangled

    B. keeping teeth healthy

    C. maintaining a clean home

    D. determining what programs are showing on television

4. A *positive / negative* impact this technology could have on society is that it makes it *easier / more difficult* for people to avoid costly and painful dental problems.

Use the diagram to answer Questions 5 and 6.

5. What information does this model of a water infrastructure provide?

    A. the flow of the system's inputs and outputs

    B. the number of people the system can support

    C. how the system would perform in a flood

6. What positive impact(s) will the construction of this water infrastructure have on the town for which it is built? Select all that apply.

    A. provide a clean and reliable water supply

    B. decrease the precipitation in the mountains

    C. create more jobs for people in the town

    D. prevent the river from flooding

7. A toothbrush is an example of a technology. Which of the following are important criteria for choosing a material for the bristles? Choose all that apply.

    A. The material comes in fashionable colors.

    B. The material is flexible and able to withstand wear.

    C. The material is able to support a large amount of weight.

    D. The material is nontoxic.

8. Which of the following is a form of technology? Select all that apply.

    A. a lollipop stick

    B. a city park

    C. a public transit system

    D. a television

Interactive Review

Complete this section to review the main concepts of the lesson.

Scientists and engineers rely on technology to study phenomena and develop solutions to engineering problems.

A. Explain how engineering and science are related.

The concept of natural and engineered systems, and models of such systems, allow scientists and engineers to study how the natural and designed worlds operate.

B. Why can models of systems represent only certain aspects of the system under study? Explain your answer.

The use of technology is influenced by factors such as scientific discoveries, cultural values, and economic conditions.

C. Identify how scientific discoveries may influence the development and use of a technology.

Small-scale and large-scale technologies can improve quality of life.

D. Give an example of how a large-scale, technology-based industry such as agriculture has benefited society.

Defining Engineering Problems

Trebuchets were medieval weapons designed to hurl objects weighing 100 kilograms a distance of up to 300 meters. Their design was based on the sling.

Explore First

Exploring the Design Process What might you do if your teacher handed you craft sticks, rubber bands, glue, and string, and asked you to build a working model of the trebuchets shown in the photo? What questions would you need to ask before starting the project?

Go online to view the digital version of the Hands-On Lab for this lesson and to download additional lab resources.

CAN YOU EXPLAIN IT?

How does the purpose of a treehouse affect how you would design and build it?

Before you start to build a treehouse, you have to figure out what structural design will allow it to serve the purpose you need it to as well as what resources you have available to you.

1. What are some questions that you might need to ask as you plan and design your treehouse?

2. Is "having access to a tree" an important factor in planning and building a treehouse? Why or why not? Explain your answer.

EVIDENCE NOTEBOOK As you explore the lesson, gather information to help explain how the treehouse's purpose is related to its design and construction.

Solving a Design Problem

Engineers use scientific principles and knowledge to address practical problems. The engineering process begins when a problem, need, or desire is identified. Scientists and engineers work to develop a solution to the problem, need, or desire. Engineering problems can be as small as designing a new type of pen or as large as designing and building a spacecraft to explore Mars. The solution can be an object, a process, or even a system involving many tools and processes.

Indoor open fires release harmful products such as soot and carbon monoxide into the air. People in the home then breathe these in, which can cause diseases.

3. Discuss Look carefully at the photo. What needs are suggested by the photo?

Engineering Begins with a Problem, a Need, or a Desire

The way people in developing countries cook food and warm their homes is a practice that often leads to serious health problems. In much of the developing world, people cook food over open fires or open stoves inside their homes. These stoves are usually poorly ventilated, which causes the fuel to burn incompletely. The fires and stoves do not usually have chimneys or stovepipes to remove smoke from the home. People who live in the house are exposed to smoke and gases from the fire. Gases, smoke, and soot from the fires cause illness and lead to the death of millions of people each year. There is a need to find practical ways to decrease this harmful exposure. Millions of lives could be saved each year. This is an example of a need that could be solved through an engineering solution.

4. To help guide an engineer to develop a safe way to meet this person's needs, identify a problem in this situation.

Questions Help Define the Engineering Problem

To develop a solution, the engineering problem must first be carefully defined. Engineers ask questions about the need. Then they conduct research to help form a precise definition of the engineering problem. For example, addressing the large-scale health problem of open fires and open stoves in the developing world requires precisely identifying the parts of the social and physical systems in which the problem occurs. Questions that help to develop a solution will also identify the systems in which the problem exists as well as other factors, including:

- the individuals or groups that are affected by the problem
- the scientific issues relevant to the problem
- potential impacts of solutions on the environment and society
- the cost-effectiveness of the design process and availability of resources
- the economic realities of the people for whom the solution will be developed

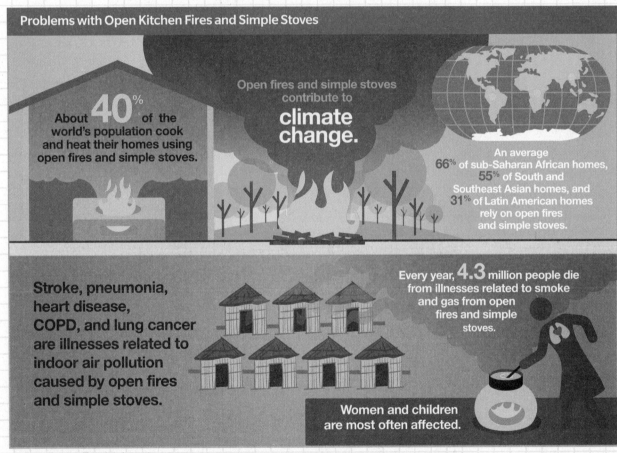

Problems with Open Kitchen Fires and Simple Stoves

About **40**% of the world's population cook and heat their homes using open fires and simple stoves.

Open fires and simple stoves contribute to **climate change.**

An average 66% of sub-Saharan African homes, 55% of South and Southeast Asian homes, and 31% of Latin American homes rely on open fires and simple stoves.

Stroke, pneumonia, heart disease, COPD, and lung cancer are illnesses related to indoor air pollution caused by open fires and simple stoves.

Every year, **4.3** million people die from illnesses related to smoke and gas from open fires and simple stoves.

Women and children are most often affected.

Source: World Health Organization Media Center, *Household Air Pollution and Health* Fact Sheet. Accessed on January 5, 2016.

5. Which questions would help define this problem? Choose all that apply.

A. How do open fires in homes cause health problems?

B. What types of buildings usually have kitchens with open fires?

C. What treatments are available for diseases caused by open fires and stoves?

D. What is the household income of families with open fires in the home?

6. **Draw** The engineering problem related to open indoor fires can be represented as a system. Illustrate the problem of open indoor fires as a system. Don't forget to add the components, processes, inputs, and outputs of this system.

Language SmArts

Describe Smartphone Requirements

Suppose you want to develop a smartphone. This is a smaller-scale problem than redesigning how millions of people around the world cook and heat their homes. Even so, the problem needs to be described in detail before designing a solution.

7. In the table, each stated problem identifies a smartphone need or desire. The precisely stated problem gives further detail about the engineering problem, which then guides a designed solution. Fill in the blank sections of the table with details that address a more specific need or desire from that of the stated problem.

Stated Problem	Precisely Stated Problem
Develop a phone that can be used by adults with special needs.	Develop a phone for use by people who are vision or hearing impaired.
Develop a phone that is "eco-friendly."	Develop a phone that contains at least 25% recycled materials.
Develop a phone that has a camera.	
Develop a way to protect a phone from damage.	
Develop a phone that is affordable.	

Defining Problems Precisely

If an engineering solution is to be useful, the problem must first be defined precisely. Imagine designing an umbrella to keep someone dry while they are walking in light rain. Your umbrella design must address the need for the umbrella to stop rain from falling on a person's head. It must also allow the person to carry other things at the same time. With these needs in mind, design criteria might include that the umbrella must be light. Therefore, the umbrella must be made of lightweight, waterproof materials. The criteria that define this umbrella design do not necessarily apply to all umbrella designs, though. Think about how criteria for a shade umbrella, or an umbrella that can stand up to hail, might be different.

Umbrellas and other rain gear must all meet specific needs of the users to be useful.

8. Which of these requirements are things you would need to consider when designing an umbrella that will keep a person dry in rain showers? Choose all that apply.

   A. fabric that is water repellent or waterproof

   B. colorful fabric print

   C. fabric that you cannot see through

   D. lightweight materials

 EVIDENCE NOTEBOOK

9. How would the engineering design problem of a treehouse to be used by young children differ from that of a treehouse to be used by teenagers? Record your evidence.

Specific Needs and Limitations Define Engineering Problems

Lighted city streets are much safer than dark streets. Until gas lamps were developed in the late 18th century, oil or kerosene lamps were used to light up streets and pathways. Then gas-fueled lights improved upon those lamps. However, gas lamps caused fires and explosions. In addition, the light from these lamps was not bright enough to light large areas. Many gas lamps were then replaced by carbon arc lights. These lights used a glowing carbon electrode that made the light very bright. They were placed high above street level. Unfortunately, arc lights needed a lot of maintenance.

The invention of the incandescent bulb improved the technology of outdoor lighting. Both streetlights and traffic signal lights used these bulbs. Today, streetlights and signal lights often use light-emitting diodes (LEDs). LEDs are more energy efficient and last much longer than incandescent bulbs. Each new streetlight design was developed to meet the changing needs of society, such as an increased focus on safety. In addition, changes to design were made as more resources became available.

Many criteria of the engineering problem of lighting up city streets have not changed in more than 100 years. Streets still need to be "brightly lit." However, today's constraints may be very different.

Criteria

Engineers usually begin defining a problem by talking with people who are experiencing the problem and who will use the solution. They might also observe the current technology in use to see how it might be improved and to find out how other people solved similar problems in the past. Improvements in street lighting, for example, came about because electrical engineers talked with people about the need for good lighting and observed the problems with the current lighting technology. The engineers developed criteria that helped define the problem. **Criteria** are the desirable features a solution should have. Criteria (singular, *criterion*) of the street lighting problem included that the lights be bright enough to light up a large area, easy to maintain, and relatively inexpensive. New lighting technologies were developed that met those criteria and that eventually replaced the older technologies.

Constraints

The limits on the design of a solution are called **constraints**. Constraints may be expressed as having a value or limit, such as, "It cannot cost more than $10 to make," or "It must withstand the force of a car crashing into it at 55 kilometers per hour." Constraints can also be limiting factors that exist because of such things as the availability of raw materials, current scientific understanding, or a country's laws. If a proposed design solution does not meet a constraint, it is unacceptable or unusable. For example, when incandescent light bulbs were invented, they were not immediately used in streetlights. They could not be used until a system to provide electrical energy to city blocks was developed. The absence of a reliable energy source was a constraint. Other constraints include time limitations, cost of materials, and environmental concerns. Precisely defining the criteria and constraints of the problem increases the likelihood of finding a successful solution.

10. Imagine you are designing streetlights for your town. The table below lists the criteria the solution should address. Score the criteria in order of importance to your design problem so you can design the best street lighting, with six being the most important and one the least important. Compare your order of criteria with your classmates'. Discuss reasons for the order of your criteria.

Criteria	Order of Importance
The lights should light up all areas of the street.	
The lights should be cost-effective to run.	
The lights should not shine into drivers' eyes.	
The light poles should be made of strong, sturdy materials.	
The lights should be made of environmentally safe materials.	
The lights should be of vintage style to match town buildings.	

11. Street lighting was originally developed to improve public safety. List the criteria from the table that relate to public safety concerns. Explain your reasoning.

Redefine Criteria and Constraints

What happens if you change the problem? When you do that, you need to define new criteria and constraints. This cyclist is trying to stay dry in the rain using an umbrella. Think about the criteria and constraints that were used to design a rain umbrella. The umbrella was a good design solution. Does the same solution work for keeping a rider dry while cycling? Think about how to define the criteria and constraints of this problem. The solution should keep a rider dry and safe while cycling in the rain.

12. Suppose you are leading a design team that is working on ways to keep cyclists dry in the rain. A standard rain umbrella creates some safety concerns. Your first task is to make a list of at least three criteria and three constraints that will help your design team to state the problem before they begin developing a solution.

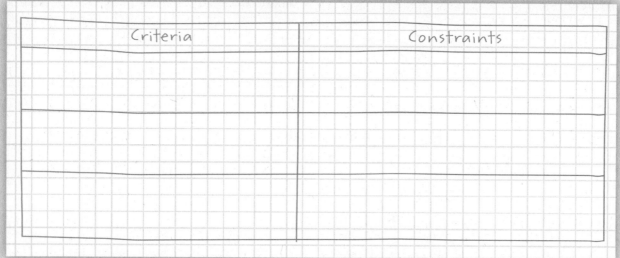

Criteria	Constraints

13. Write a precisely defined engineering problem for a design solution that protects a bicycle rider from the rain. Use the criteria and constraints that you identified above.

_____
_____
_____
_____
_____
_____
_____

© Houghton Mifflin Harcourt Publishing Company • Image Credits: ©Vivek Prakash/Reuters/Corbis

Researching to Define Engineering Problems

Soapbox car racing, also known as gravity racing, is an annual event in many places in the United States. In these races, sleek, motorless cars race downhill. Drivers race against each other or against the clock. The cars do not have engines, but they can reach speeds of up to 56 kilometers per hour (35 miles per hour). Gravity racing events began in the United States in the mid-1930s and were open to male racers only. Since 1971, female drivers have also raced. Anyone between the ages of 7 and 20 years old can compete in these annual races. The challenge for participants to build the fastest car possible is a good example of the need to precisely define an engineering problem.

Imagine that you have entered a soapbox car race. You will use the engineering design process to state the engineering problem and then design a solution.

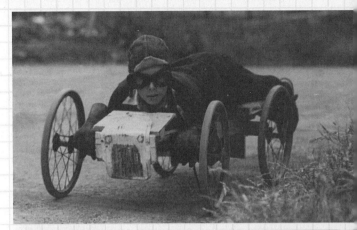

The design of soapbox cars, also called gravity racer cars, has changed over time. The availability of different materials and safety concerns are just two influences on the design.

14. Research will help you identify how this problem was addressed in the past. Your goal is to make the fastest car along the given course. First, identify questions you need to answer to precisely define the design problem you face. Then, identify the information and data you will need to plan the next steps of the design process.

Questions	Information and Data Needed

Engineering Problems Can Be Reframed

An engineering question builds on initial research. Sometimes, though, new information may require engineers to change, or reframe, the engineering question. This new information may mean that the question needs to be restated and a new solution proposed.

When Criteria or Constraints Change

Reframing may be needed when there is a change in the criteria or constraints of a problem as well. For example, after your research on the soapbox car, you might find out that cars are scored on appearance as well as speed. This new criterion requires that you reframe your question. A new constraint, such as a change in the maximum width of the car body, means your design question needs to be reframed. Your design problem now has different dimensions that affect the amount of material needed.

Reframing an engineering problem in the early stages of the solution development is better than doing so later, after the testing phase begins. Defining the engineering problem so that it best describes the problem without having to consider time or cost would be ideal. But it usually does not work that way. Engineers need to research production costs, schedules, market pressures, new scientific discoveries, and customer likes and dislikes before they can clearly define engineering problems. This type of research helps identify the criteria and constraints for a successful solution.

These wooden derby cars look different from one another, but they all were designed to meet the same constraints and criteria to make the race fair.

15. After you start planning the design for your soapbox racecar, you find out that the maximum weight for the car has changed. What new information do you need and what changes to your design plan would you have to make in order for your design to fit the new constraint?

 EVIDENCE NOTEBOOK

16. Suppose the treehouse was at first meant to be big enough for three people, but then the builder decided it should fit five instead. How would this change affect the treehouse design? Record your evidence.

© Houghton Mifflin Harcourt Publishing Company • Image Credits: ©Lynn Seeden/E+/ Getty Images

Hands-On Lab
Design a Model Car, Part 1

Define an engineering problem for a model car design.

You will build a model car in class over several lessons. Your challenge is to build a car that will travel the farthest after being rolled down a three-foot-long ramp slanted at 30°. In developing a solution, you need to think about how limits such as the materials available to you, the time you have to complete the solution, and scientific principles will affect the available solutions.

Here are the criteria and constraints that define your design problem:

- The mass of the car must not be greater than 120 g.
- The length of the car must not be greater than 15 cm.
- The width of the car must not be greater than 7 cm.
- The car must have a 4.5-cm distance between the axles.
- The car must have a 1-cm clearance underneath the body.
- The car must be made only from materials provided by your teacher.
- The car body may have any shape.
- The car must be reusable.
- The car must have four wheels.
- The axles, axle housing, and wheels supplied with the kit must be used.
- The axles, axle housing, and wheels may not be changed in any way.
- The only weights that may be added to the car are washers supplied in the kit.
- The car should include a to-scale model driver.

> **MATERIALS**
> - corrugated cardboard
> - digital scale
> - measuring tape
> - metal washers (weights)
> - smoothie straws
> - scissors
> - tape
> - wooden axles (2)
> - wooden wheels (4)
>
>

Procedure

STEP 1 Criteria are features the solution should have. Constraints are the limitations the designers need to work within. What are the criteria of this design problem?

STEP 2 Identify the constraints of the design problem.

STEP 3 Clearly state the design problem. What need will the design address?

STEP 4 Think of at least three body plans for the shape of your car. Choose the one most likely to meet the criteria. Give reasons for your decision.

Analysis

STEP 5 **Do the Math** As part of your design, you will cut out a paper driver to attach to the top of your car. You want the driver to be correctly scaled to the car. The length of a typical soapbox derby car is 1.2 m. Your model soapbox derby car is 14 cm long. To the nearest centimeter, how tall should your model driver be in order to represent a 1.67-m-tall driver?

STEP 6 Why is it important to define the design problem more precisely than "design a small, fast model car"? Explain your answer using what you have learned about the engineering design process.

Reframe an Engineering Problem

If the race's rules were changed to say that each car should have three wheels instead of four, you would need to reframe the problem. Your design would have to include changing the locations of the wheels and changing the car's weight distribution.

17. Suppose a student wants to use the same car design in a new competition. She discovers that the guidelines for the new competition are different. For each new guideline, indicate whether reframing of the problem will be needed.

> A. Reframing may be needed
> B. Reframing not needed

_____ The car must have a 2-cm clearance below the body.

_____ Wheels may be made from any material.

_____ To prevent accidental poisoning, lead weights cannot be used in the car design.

Continue Your Exploration

Name: _____   **Date:** _____

Check out the path below or go online to choose one of the other paths shown.

Redefining a Design Problem

- **Learning from Design Failures**
- **Hands-On Labs** 🖐
- **Propose Your Own Path**

Go online to choose one of these other paths.

Harnessing Wind Energy

Wind is a renewable energy source because it is generated continually. Wind turbines use wind to produce electrical energy. In many places around the world, giant windmill-like turbines stand on top of ridges, in wide prairies, or offshore. In these fairly isolated places, the structures do not generally interfere with the lives of people. These large turbines are not designed for use in urban areas because they take up a lot of space and require strong winds to move their blades.

Adjustments for Societal and Environmental Needs

How could you use engineering design to develop a way to harness wind energy in a city while meeting the constraints of urban needs? One solution is the Wind Tree® shown in the picture. This artificial tree has "leaves" that are lightweight wind turbines. Generators and cables are located inside the branches and trunk. The Wind Tree silently produces electric power even in a light breeze.

Jérôme Michaud-Larivière, a French entrepreneur, developed the design after observing how even a very light wind rustled the leaves on trees. Michaud-Larivière wondered whether a wind-energy device based on several mini spinning turbines could generate enough energy to be useful in cities. The Wind Tree design has a relatively low power output of about 3.1 kW from light breezes when compared to the 2.5 to 3 MW output of traditional, large, land-based turbines. Michaud-Larivière suggested that a street lined with Wind Trees could power city streetlights or help offset the power use of nearby buildings.

Continue Your Exploration

1. Explain, in terms of criteria and constraints, why the design of a traditional wind turbine might not be suitable for use in a city.

2. For the mini turbines to operate properly, which of the following criteria are important in choosing the material for their construction?

   A. lightweight

   B. recycled

   C. realistic leaf colors

   D. attracts insects

   E. waterproof

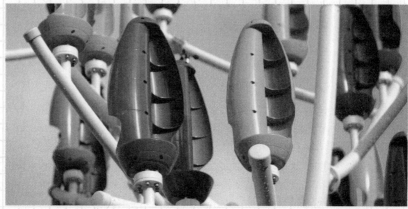

The "leaves" of Wind Trees are miniature turbines. They can move in light breezes.

3. Do the Math The kilowatt (kW) is a measure of power. Wind Tree turbines have a power output of 3.1 kW. The lightweight leaf turbines can move in light breezes. A traditional, large wind turbine can have a power output of up to 3 megawatts (MW), but strong winds are needed to move the large turbines. The large turbines are more powerful machines than the smaller Wind Trees because they can do the same amount of work over a shorter period of time.

How many Wind Trees would it take to match the power output of five large turbines? Remember that 1 MW equals 1,000 kW. Round your answer to the nearest whole number.

4. **Collaborate** As a team, learn about how changes to environmental and health laws have affected issues that engineers and designers of city infrastructure technologies deal with today.

Can You Explain It?

Name: _____   Date: _____

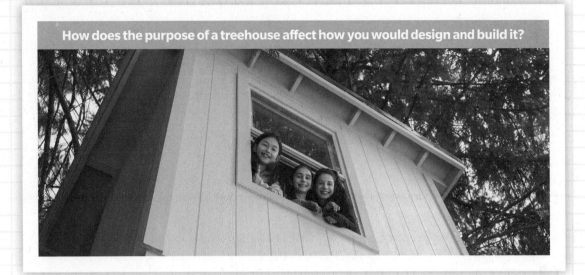

How does the purpose of a treehouse affect how you would design and build it?

EVIDENCE NOTEBOOK

Refer to the notes in your Evidence Notebook to help you explain how the purpose of a treehouse is related to its design.

1. State your claim. Make sure your claim fully explains how the purpose of an object is related to the engineering problem of designing and building it.

2. Summarize the evidence you have gathered to support your claim and explain your reasoning.

Checkpoints

Answer the following questions to check your understanding of the lesson.

Use the photo to answer Questions 3 and 4.

3. The ladder for this treehouse has been removed because the wood was rotting. You need to design a new way to get into the treehouse. Which questions would help define this engineering problem more precisely? Choose all that apply.

   A. How much do the users of the treehouse weigh?

   B. What materials and tools can I use?

   C. Is the rope on the tire swing strong enough to be safe if two people are on the tire?

   D. Is there a way to close the window for privacy?

4. Each statement below refers to the engineering problem of designing and building a new way of accessing the treehouse. In the blank cells of the table, classify each statement as a criterion, a constraint, or neither a criterion nor a constraint of the problem.

Availability of tools and boards	
Desire to remove treehouse access after entry into it	
Treehouse to be made of wood	
Availability of roofing materials	

Use the photo to answer Questions 5 and 6.

5. The candles in the photo are a solution to a defined engineering problem. What problem do these candles solve?

   A. Warm up the room for the diners.

   B. Light up the entrance to the room.

   C. Light up the dinner table without relying on electricity.

   D. Light up the table brightly enough to read a book.

6. One hundred fifty years ago, the solution illustrated in this photo was the best solution to the need to provide light in a home at night. Today, it is not the best solution to this problem. What has likely changed? Choose all that apply.

   A. Most modern houses have electric lighting.

   B. Electric lights are safer and more convenient.

   C. Most modern houses have indoor plumbing.

© Houghton Mifflin Harcourt Publishing Company • Image Credits: (t) ©Anne Clark/E+/Getty Images; (b) ©John Warburton–Lee Photography/AWL Images/Getty Images

Interactive Review

Complete this section to review the main concepts of the lesson.

A well-defined engineering problem identifies the needs or wants it is intended to address.

A. Why is it important to identify the right questions when developing a solution to an engineering design problem?

In order to develop a usable solution to a design problem, the problem must state specific needs and limitations that must be met.

B. How are criteria and constraints used to make a precisely stated solution to an engineering design problem?

Researching how similar problems were addressed in the past can help engineers define the design problem precisely.

C. Sometimes an engineering problem must be reframed. What might occur that would require an engineer to reframe an engineering problem?

Developing and Testing Solutions

Thomas Edison did not invent the incandescent light bulb, but he improved its design and made it more practical.

Explore First

Comparing Solutions Obtain a wooden pencil and a mechanical pencil. Identify a specific task for which you can test both pencil designs, such as consistency in drawing lines. Carry out your test and record the results. How well did each pencil do in the test?

Go online to view the digital version of the Hands-On Lab for this lesson and to download additional lab resources.

CAN YOU EXPLAIN IT?

How can you develop and test ways to get a kite out of a tree?

Oh no! Your favorite kite is caught in a tree and its string is tangled in the branches. What can you do to free it? A workable solution is one that keeps you safe and keeps the kite and tree as intact as possible.

1. Provide an example of a criterion and a constraint of this problem.

2. How might the material the kite is made of affect the solution of retrieving it from the tree?

EVIDENCE NOTEBOOK As you explore this lesson, gather information to explain how to develop a solution to the problem of the kite stuck in the tree.

Developing Solutions

There is not always one clear solution to an engineering problem. After the criteria and constraints of a problem have been defined, engineers brainstorm ideas for solutions. After the brainstorming step, you may have several design solutions you think will meet the criteria and constraints. You can test one or two of the solutions to see if that is true. You may decide to modify or combine solutions to develop a better solution.

For example, imagine your class is planning a field trip to study a stream ecosystem. Part of your study includes analyzing the water quality of the stream using delicate electronic equipment. Eight sets of equipment will be used by the class. It is not possible to drive directly to the stream, so you need to carry the fragile equipment from the school bus. The distance from the bus parking lot to the stream is a quarter mile. Defining this transportation problem using criteria and constraints and then prioritizing the criteria will help develop a solution.

After identifying the important requirements of a problem, you can use brainstorming and planning to develop solutions.

3. Using a scale of 1–5, identify the importance of each criterion of the problem, with 5 being the most important and 1 being the least important.

	Rating (1-5)
Must be easy for a student to use, carry, or hold	
Must not damage the electronic equipment	
Must be reusable	
Must be inexpensive	
Must not be damaged by being used on a rocky trail	

4. **Discuss** Before the field trip, your class discusses the best ways to move the equipment. One student suggests using the janitor's hand-pulled, metal wagon. You test this idea and discover that the equipment would get dented if placed on the metal bottom of the wagon. What could you do to address the issue with denting?

Brainstorm Solutions

One way to generate ideas is to brainstorm with other people. When you work with others to think about and generate ideas quickly, you are **brainstorming**. You can brainstorm in different ways, but the most important thing is to suggest as many ideas as possible while avoiding judgments about any suggestions. The goal of a brainstorming session is to identify many solutions in order to find a few to refine further. Some ideas may turn out to be unusable, but brainstorming is not the time to figure out which ideas may or may not work. Brainstorming many ideas can often result in a much better solution than starting with a single idea alone. Considering only one option from the start can limit the creativity of the solution.

Brainstorming sessions can generate a lot of ideas.

5. The goal of brainstorming is to generate a number of possible solutions. Which statements are advantages of brainstorming many ideas instead of focusing on one initial solution? Choose all that apply.

   A. Multiple ideas increase the chance of finding a workable solution.

   B. Larger groups can reach a conclusion about a solution faster.

   C. Several different ideas might combine to form a better solution.

   D. New ideas may be generated from others' suggestions.

The Importance of Being Open-Minded

All ideas are considered valuable during brainstorming sessions. The ideas proposed in a brainstorming session are not completely random, though. As possible solutions are suggested, it is important that the criteria and constraints are kept in mind. One very important constraint to any solution is the budget. A solution such as using drones to carry the equipment to the stream is not a workable solution. It would be too expensive for the school to afford. However, if each student already had their own drone they could bring with them, using drones might be a workable solution.

When brainstorming, participants also have background knowledge about how similar problems were solved in the past. They can also use what they know of scientific principles and legal requirements related to the problem and the proposed solutions. For example, there are several laws that restrict the use of drones. If the use of drones is prohibited in the area where the field trip is, then it is not a suitable solution even if the school could afford to use them.

The Importance of Background Research

In order to find the best design solution for an engineering problem, research is also needed. If you jump straight into brainstorming without researching solutions that are already available or how similar problems were solved in the past, you do extra work and waste time. Part of the solution may already exist. By researching the problem, you start with a background of knowledge. Sometimes background research helps reframe the problem so that it is better focused. Research into a solution often continues after ideas are generated by brainstorming.

Use Decision-Making Tools

Some of the brainstormed solutions may not meet all the criteria of the problem, or maybe all of the solutions meet the criteria. Some solutions may be more effective or safer than others. Possible solutions are evaluated against the criteria and constraints. Less-effective solutions are rejected, and the remaining solutions are refined.

Workable solutions must meet the constraints of the problem. If a solution does not meet a constraint, it is eliminated. For example, renting a satellite phone to send data home from a field trip would be beyond your budget. But for a research team in a ship on the ocean, a satellite phone might be the best option to stay in contact with others.

Decision Matrix

Several decision-making tools can help you choose among the solutions to find the best option. A **decision matrix** is one tool for evaluating several options at the same time. In a decision matrix, each criterion is assigned a number that rates its importance in a successful design solution. For example, suppose students are asked to design a container to take soup to school for lunch. After brainstorming solutions, they can use a decision matrix like the one below to rate each idea to see which one best meets the criteria. In this example, students have decided that "does not leak" is the most important criterion of the design solution. They assign it a rating of five points.

The higher the point value, the more important the criterion is to a successful solution. Each solution is then scored on how well it meets each criterion. Points are awarded for each solution up to, but no more than, the maximum rating given to the criterion. The result is a numerical ranking of the proposed solutions based on the importance of the criterion for a successful solution. The solution that has the highest total score is the one that best addresses the problem.

Criteria	Rating (1–5)	Soup Container Solutions			
		Plastic container with screw-on lid	Foam container	Glass jar with lid	Plastic zipper bag
Easy to reuse	4	4	2	3	1
Does not leak	5	5	3	4	2
Not expensive	4	2	4	1	4
Unlikely to break	3	3	2	1	1
Totals		14	11	9	8

6. Which solution meets the criteria the best? Explain how the matrix provides useful information for evaluating the solution to the problem.

EVIDENCE NOTEBOOK

7. Brainstorming ways to get the kite out of the tree might lead to many potential solutions. How can you determine which solutions are most likely to succeed? Record your evidence.

Tradeoffs

Making a decision about the best solution nearly always involves making a tradeoff. In the case of the best container for carrying soup, the plastic container with the screw-on lid was the best solution. But the plastic foam container is cheaper and does a good job of not leaking, so you might choose it instead, because it would be a more affordable option for you. A tradeoff involves giving up something you like about one solution in order to have a more desirable feature in another solution.

Risk-Benefit Analysis

Another tool engineers often use to evaluate options is a risk-benefit analysis. A **risk-benefit analysis** compares the risks, or unfavorable effects, of a solution, to the benefits, or favorable effects. A solution that has greater benefits and fewer risks is favored over one with fewer benefits and greater risks. For example, x-ray machines are tools that doctors use to see inside the body to evaluate and diagnose health problems. However, as x-rays pass through the body, they can damage living cells. Medical x-rays expose patients to very small doses of radiation. The risk of harm to cells is considered much smaller than the benefit of being able to diagnose health problems.

Select Promising Solutions

8. You have drawn a decision matrix to help assess how well several solutions meet the criteria of the problem: "What item is best to bring to the beach to sit on?" Five criteria and four solutions are written into the decision matrix. Your next step is to rank the importance of each criterion for a successful solution. Then, fill out the matrix by awarding points to each solution based on how well it meets each criterion.

Criteria	Rating (1–5)	Solutions			
		Folding camp chair	Inflatable beach float	Beach towel	Metal patio chair
Not expensive					
Easy to carry					
Washable					
Comfortable for sitting					
Waterproof materials					
Totals					

Which solution was the "best"? Explain your answer.

_____

_____

What type of tradeoff would you need to make if you were to choose the second-highest-scoring solution? Explain your answers.

_____

_____

_____

Evaluating Solutions

A decision matrix helps you evaluate possible solutions. However, it does not provide every answer to address a design problem. The top-rated proposed solution to taking soup to school for lunch is the plastic container with the screw-on lid. This may well be the best way to carry soup to school. However, there are additional things you need to do before deciding this is the best solution. Solutions that seem to be perfectly workable sometimes do not actually solve the problem. After a solution or several possible solutions to a problem are identified, they are tested to identify whether they meet all the criteria and constraints of the problem. Testing several types of screw-top plastic containers that hold different volumes or have different styles of screw-top lids will help identify the best solution to your problem.

A universal testing machine is used to test the tensile strength and compressive strength of materials. It can apply pulling (tensile) or pushing (compressive) forces on the test material. This fabric is undergoing a tensile strength test.

Explore Online

9. An engineering team proposes a new water-resistant fabric for use in backpacks. Several different fabrics have been recommended. Why would it be helpful for the team to test each of the proposals before manufacturing the new backpacks? Choose all answers that apply.

   A. Testing can help engineers determine whether one option is better than the others.

   B. Engineers can use test results to confirm whether the fabrics actually work in real situations.

   C. Testing may help engineers discover ways in which the fabrics perform better or worse than predicted.

   D. Engineers may use testing to obtain information on ways to improve the performance of the fabrics.

Test Solutions

Similar to scientists, engineers rely on reproducible data in order to make and defend conclusions. Analyzing test results helps engineers identify which solution is best and whether the best solution solves the problem. In order to be useful, a test should measure one variable at a time. This provides information to evaluate the proposed solution and often leads to improvements in the design.

Some tests can be carried out using the solution exactly as proposed. For example, you can test which container best holds soup by testing the containers themselves. Sometimes, however, the actual solution cannot be tested directly. For example, engineers designing a large suspension bridge cannot build the bridge and then test it to see whether the design was right. Instead, they test a model of the bridge. A working test model of a solution is called a **prototype**. Engineers use prototypes during the design process to test the design and make improvements to it.

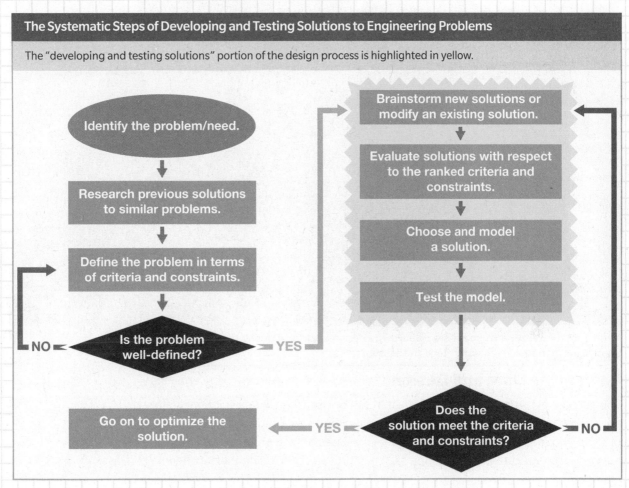

The Systematic Steps of Developing and Testing Solutions to Engineering Problems

The "developing and testing solutions" portion of the design process is highlighted in yellow.

Identify the problem/need.

Research previous solutions to similar problems.

Define the problem in terms of criteria and constraints.

Is the problem well-defined? — NO / YES

Brainstorm new solutions or modify an existing solution.

Evaluate solutions with respect to the ranked criteria and constraints.

Choose and model a solution.

Test the model.

Does the solution meet the criteria and constraints? — YES / NO

Go on to optimize the solution.

10. A decision matrix can be used to narrow down solutions. Often two or three solutions appear to be equally promising. When that happens it will be important to test each of the top designs to see which ones best meet the criteria. Why is it important that each of the top designs be tested in the same way?

Evaluate Test Data

Once engineers use a design matrix to identify the top two or three solutions, they build prototypes for testing. Many tests provide numerical data that can be compared mathematically. Every aspect of a solution can be tested, including the cost of materials and the time needed to implement the solution. These students are testing a parachute design model to see how long it takes to drop from the balcony. They want to develop a parachute that takes the longest time possible to drop. They will compare data from several tests and different designs to identify the best solution.

An important part of evaluating a design is building a design model and testing the model to measure the design's performance against criteria and constraints.

Review the Data and Design

The purpose of testing is to provide data that can be used to evaluate solutions. After data collection, each solution is evaluated against the criteria and constraints. The data provide evidence about the strengths and weaknesses of each proposed solution. The data may also indicate ways a solution can be improved upon. Using the data, team members can then provide constructive criticism of each solution. This analysis, which is based on evidence, helps to improve solutions.

11. Sometimes parts of different solutions can be combined to make a better solution. What benefit does this offer? Choose all that apply.

A. It allows for the best part of each solution to be used in a final design.

B. It gives the design team time to redefine the problem.

C. It allows the designers to meet customer demands for new designs every year.

D. It allows a solution to be developed that is better than earlier solutions.

E. It allows each test variable to be tested fully in each test model.

© Houghton Mifflin Harcourt Publishing Company • Image Credits: ©Houghton Mifflin Harcourt

Do the Math
Evaluate Parachute Designs

A group of students is designing a parachute system to drop an egg from a height of 3 meters without breaking the egg. The purpose of the first test was to compare the effectiveness of different parachute materials and sizes. To avoid making a mess, they tested their designs using a wooden block with a mass similar to that of an egg.

The variables in the tests were the parachute material and the parachute size. All of the test designs were dropped from the same point on the balcony using the same mass. The table below shows the averaged results after testing each design three times. Students then evaluated the data to determine which solution would be most likely to keep an egg from breaking.

Type of Parachute Material	Area of Parachute (cm²)	Time to Reach the Floor (s)
Cloth	500	1.7
Cloth	1,000	2.2
Plastic film	500	2.7
Plastic film	1,000	3.5
Paper	500	2.0
Paper	1,000	2.5

12. Based on the evidence from the tests, make a recommendation about the type of material the students should use for their parachute. Explain your reasoning.

13. A wooden block was used as a model egg in evaluating the parachute design. What could the students do to determine whether their design will work on a real egg?

EVIDENCE NOTEBOOK

14. Suppose you have identified two promising potential solutions to the kite problem. How can you further evaluate and choose a solution? Record your evidence.

Hands-On Lab
Design a Model Car, Part 2

Propose design solutions based on your earlier work defining the problem.

You are designing and building a model car over several sessions. In Part 1, you defined the engineering problem. Now, in Part 2, you will propose design solutions. Later, in Part 3, you will evaluate the proposed solutions against the criteria.

Your challenge is to build a model car using the supplied materials and specifications. Refer to the criteria, constraints, and materials listed in Part 1 of this Hands-On Lab, which is in Lesson 2.

MATERIALS
• See materials from Design a Model Car, Part 1

Procedure

STEP 1 Brainstorm with your group to come up with several car designs to meet the challenge.

STEP 2 Identify three car design options that you want to explore further. Analyze how well these three design options meet the criteria of the problem using a decision matrix similar to the one shown below. Three criteria are listed in the sample matrix.

STEP 3 On a separate piece of paper, draw a decision matrix similar to the one shown below that lists the criteria of your design. Then, rank the importance of each criterion for the solution to be acceptable using a scale of 1 to 5 for each criterion with 1 meaning "least important" and 5 meaning "most important." Then, score each solution based on how well it meets each ranked criterion. Remember that points are awarded for each criterion up to, but no more than, the maximum value given to that criterion.

Criteria	Rating (1–5)	Solutions		
		Car design 1	Car design 2	Car design 3
Max mass of 120 g				
Has four wheels				
Is reusable				
Totals				

STEP 4 **Draw** Based on your decision matrix, choose the design solution that scores the highest. This is the design that best meets the criteria. Draw a sketch of the design on a separate sheet of paper. Then, build your chosen design! Remember, you may use only the materials supplied by your teacher to build the car.

STEP 5 Any complex design project involves carrying out a number of tests to see how variables affect the performance of the design. There are several design variables that may affect the performance of the car. Some of these variables include the shape of the car, the weight of the car, and the location of the weights (washers) on the body.

Choose one variable to test to identify how it affects the distance traveled by the car. Remember to check the race specifications to be sure you are testing only values of the variables that are within the allowed range for your car.

STEP 6 Design a test to evaluate the effect of the one variable on the distance the car travels. Explain how the test will be carried out.

STEP 7 Using a test ramp, conduct the test. Record your results on a separate sheet of paper.

STEP 8 You may, if time allows, identify and test another variable to see how it affects your car's performance.

Analysis

STEP 9 On a separate sheet of paper, draw a graph showing the relationship between the change in your variable and the distance the car traveled. Draw a graph for each variable tested. Remember to label the axes. Evaluate the effect of the variable on the distance traveled. State a conclusion about the effect the variable had on the distance the car traveled.

STEP 10 Suppose one member of your group suggests that to save time, two variables that may affect the distance traveled can be tested at the same time. Is this an acceptable way to test a design solution? Explain your answer.

STEP 11 Ideally, several tests that investigate the effect of different variables on the performance of the design solution are carried out. What is the purpose of carrying out so many tests on a design solution?

Engage in Argument from Evidence

Analysis of solutions includes using data to make suggestions for improvement to the solution. A conclusion that is not supported by data is not useful to the design process.

After deciding to use a plastic film parachute to slow the fall of an egg, students built different parachute sizes and tested them by dropping the parachute and mass from a height of 3 m. Each parachute was tested three times. The average time to reach the floor is recorded in the table.

Area of Parachute (cm²)	Time to Reach the Floor (s)
100	1.0
250	1.5
500	2.7
1,000	3.5
1,500	2.7
2,000	2.1

15. One student argued that a parachute with a larger area is always better because it provides more air resistance. Explain how the data supports or does not support that argument.

_____

_____

_____

_____

_____

16. What size parachute would be the most suited to slow the fall of an egg? Use data from the table to support your conclusion.

_____

_____

_____

_____

17. Why is systematic testing of possible solutions needed before choosing a design to refine?

_____

_____

_____

_____

_____

Continue Your Exploration

Name: _____   Date: _____

Check out the path below or go online to choose one of the other paths shown.

| Building on Earlier Solutions | • Using Data to Make Informed Decisions • Hands-On Labs 🖐 • Propose Your Own Path | Go online to choose one of these other paths. |

Design of the Incandescent Light Bulb

The incandescent light bulb is a common technology. Thomas Edison is often thought of as its inventor, but he did not invent it. However, in 1878, he and his team developed the first practical and commercially successful incandescent bulb.

Edison approached the design of the light bulb as an engineering problem. He needed to develop a bulb that would produce enough light but not burn out quickly. He and his assistants tested thousands of materials and setups. In fact, Edison stated, "I have not failed. I've just found 10,000 ways that won't work."

Many Solutions Tested

Some of Edison's designs used a filament. A bulb filament is the part that lights up. It is a thin wire through which electric current flows. Some of the filament designs did not work because the material did not carry enough electric current. Others worked for a short period and then burned out. By combining what Edison and his team had learned in many tests, they eventually found a solution—a metal filament in a vacuum tube.

Thomas Edison speaks with a researcher in his lab in 1906.

Edison's success in making a light bulb included using data collected from numerous experiments to help brainstorm new ideas. His team tested many different materials and configurations to find a workable solution. Brainstorming was part of the process, although Edison and his team would not have used that term. By remaining open to many possible solutions and knowing that "failure" was an important part of the learning process, Edison eventually solved the problem.

57

Continue Your Exploration

1. How would the usefulness of the incandescent bulb have been affected if electrical supply systems had not been developed?

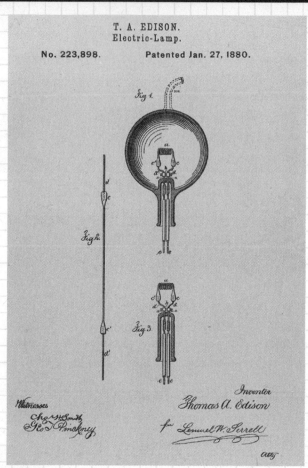

T. A. EDISON.
Electric-Lamp.

No. 223,898.   Patented Jan. 27, 1880.

2. Explain how Edison and his team used test evidence from failed tests to find the best material for the light bulb elements.

This is Edison's patent filing for his light bulb design. A patent is a license from the government that legally protects an invention from being copied or sold by others.

3. The term *brainstorming* was not used in Edison's time, but the descriptions of his research imply that his team used the technique. What aspect of Edison's research supports this idea?

4. **Collaborate** Work with your group to research the solution to an engineering problem that has had an impact on society. Find out who developed the first workable solution and how ideas were tested during the design process.

Can You Explain It?

Name: _____   **Date:** _____

How can you develop and test ways to get a kite out of a tree?

EVIDENCE NOTEBOOK

Refer to the notes in your Evidence Notebook to help you construct an explanation for how to develop solutions for a kite stuck in a tree.

1. State your claim. Make sure your claim fully explains how to develop and evaluate potential solutions to the problem.

2. Summarize the evidence you have gathered to support your claim and explain your reasoning.

Checkpoints

Answer the following questions to check your understanding of the lesson.

Use the photo to answer Question 3.

3. How does ranking criteria help designers develop a better helmet? Choose all that apply.

   A. It automatically ranks constraints because they are the same as criteria.

   B. It identifies the most important criteria that a solution must meet.

   C. It helps in assessing several solutions that meet the criteria of the problem.

   D. It helps to eliminate solutions that do not meet the constraints.

Use the photo to answer Question 4.

4. Calligraphy requires a writing tool that can make very precise and fine marks. Identify things you would do to help identify the best calligraphy pen from several different types of pens. Choose all that apply.

   A. Identify whether each pen meets the criteria of your calligraphy writing problem.

   B. Identify pens that do not meet the constraints of your writing problem.

   C. Test the pens to see which one best meets the criteria.

   D. Rank the criteria of the problem in their order of importance for a successful solution.

5. Why is using models an important part of the testing process? Choose all that apply.

   A. They allow designers to brainstorm better ideas.

   B. They allow the design solution to be tested when the actual solution itself cannot be tested.

   C. They allow design solutions to be tested in a systematic way.

   D. Their use provides engineers with lots of data to evaluate the performance of a possible design solution.

6. A team of students is designing a robot to compete in a race. They select three ideas to develop further. Which statements describe the steps the team might take to identify the best robot design? Choose all that apply.

   A. Build and test models of each design.

   B. Choose a team leader who will choose the design to build.

   C. Evaluate test data for each design and see how each one meets the criteria and constraints of the problem.

   D. Use the design that looks the best and discard the others.

Interactive Review

41

Complete this section to review the main concepts of the lesson.

Engineering solutions are developed by proposing ideas and then comparing how well those ideas meet the criteria and constraints of the problem.

A. How is a decision matrix useful during the development of a solution to an engineering design problem?

Testing provides data that can be used to rank proposed solutions and evaluate the effects of changes to design solutions.

B. Why is analyzing data from tests important to improving a design solution?

Optimizing Solutions

The Akashi Kaikyō Bridge spans 3.9 km (2.43 miles) across the Akashi Strait. It links the city of Kobe with Awaji-shima Island in Japan. It is the longest suspension bridge in the world.

Explore First

Avoiding Cracked Screens Conduct a class survey to gather data on what causes the screens of students' phones to crack. Identify whether the phones had covers or screen covers when they fell or cracked. Are there cover designs that are more successful at protecting the screen?

CAN YOU EXPLAIN IT?

How can you determine the best way to keep plates from breaking on hard floors?

Most kitchens have hard floors, which are easy to clean. However, if a plate is dropped on a hard surface, it will break. Several solutions to prevent breaking plates are available. Identifying the solution that works the best and making it better is called optimization.

1. Imagine you are a chef in a busy kitchen. You need to reduce the number of plates that break because broken plates are a safety hazard and they need to be replaced. What are five potential solutions to this problem?

2. Choose the solution you think might work best for the problem above. Identify ways you could test it in order to make it the best solution for your problem.

 EVIDENCE NOTEBOOK As you explore this lesson, gather information to help explain how you would choose a solution for this problem.

Improving a Promising Design Solution

Treats, such as muffins, are designed to taste delicious. Some muffin recipes make large and fluffy muffins. Other recipes make smaller, denser muffins. Each recipe uses different amounts of ingredients, such as baking powder, that make them light or dense. Imagine that you found a recipe for blueberry muffins that is rated as "delicious" by reviewers. You want to make the muffins for a party. Your design problem is to create muffins that are bite-sized and do not crumble, so you want to test the recipe first. If the muffins are too dense, people might not like them. If they are too fluffy, they will likely break apart when people bite into them. You follow the recipe. Then you test your design by tasting a muffin. It falls apart. It is too crumbly. It needs to be denser.

Build on the Most Promising Design

You have a design solution (a recipe), but it is currently not the best solution to your problem (to make small muffins for the party). You need to experiment to optimize the recipe. You decide to make several batches of muffins and change the amount of baking powder in each batch. The only way to know what such changes might do is to test the recipes and check the results.

Design optimization is the process of making an object or system as effective and useful as possible. A design solution, whether it is a blueberry muffin recipe or an engine part, is always tested to determine whether it is a better solution than any of those previously tested. Improvements to a design are made in response to test results.

Testing the recipe and modifying it based on your results will lead to a recipe that best meets your needs.

3. Optimizing a design solution always involves testing the modified solution. Why is it helpful to replicate these tests? Use the example of the muffin recipe in your answer.

Make Tradeoffs

Analysis of test data gives information about how a solution will perform in real-life situations. Data analysis also helps determine whether a design solution can be built within a given budget or whether it can meet constraints on the retail cost. These types of analyses do not always provide definite answers as to which solution is best. Sometimes tradeoffs are necessary to come to the solution that is most likely to meet the criteria. For example, a metal case for a cell phone might increase the lifetime of the phone. However, a plastic case is much less expensive and is lighter in weight, which customers prefer. The designer must identify which criteria are most important, such as "lower cost" and "lighter weight," instead of "a longer lifetime," before moving to the next steps in the optimization process. In this example, the designer might choose to go with a plastic case. The designer has made a tradeoff, giving up a longer lifetime for the product in favor of a lower cost and a lighter weight.

4. Why is making a tradeoff an important part of optimizing a design? Choose all that apply.

A. It helps to identify more criteria.

B. It gets rid of unnecessary constraints.

C. It helps identify what the designer needs to do next.

D. It helps identify the most important features the design solution should have.

Test Models

In selecting the best solution, engineers often perform tests on a type of model called a prototype. A **prototype** is a test model of a design solution. Prototypes are usually the first working models of a new design. They are built for testing and may be shown to others to get feedback for improving the design. Sometimes a prototype is an actual working example of the design, but often, especially for large or complex designs, it may be a scale model of the object or even just a part of the object.

Prototypes can also be tested for design flaws, safety, and ease of use. These tests help ensure that everything works the way it should and that customers can figure out how to make it work. Otherwise, the product may become an expensive design failure.

Engineers use prototypes to identify precise changes to the design. This shoe prototype was printed using a 3D printer.

Evaluate Advantages and Disadvantages

After testing, solutions can be further evaluated using tools such as a cost-benefit analysis. A *cost-benefit analysis* is a method of identifying the strengths and weaknesses of a design solution. One example is comparing the production costs to the benefits the solution offers. A cost-benefit analysis helps determine which solutions are most promising. This kind of analysis can be used to develop and refine solutions at several points throughout the design process.

Do the Math
Use Math for Design Improvement

In order to minimize costs for the manufacturer, processed food is often packaged in containers that allow the maximum storage volume but use the minimum amount of material. The best design solution for a cereal box can be chosen by calculating the box dimensions that best meet the criteria of maximum volume and the least amount of cardboard.

The table below shows some calculations that engineers made while creating a cereal box. Your task is to find the cereal box size that has the maximum volume and the least surface area (has the largest volume-to-surface-area ratio), or that uses the least amount of cardboard. The design criteria are as follows:

- The volume must be between 3,400 cm³ and 3,425 cm³.
- The height must be between 25 cm and 27 cm.
- The length must be between 18 cm and 20 cm.
- The width must be between 6 cm and 8 cm.

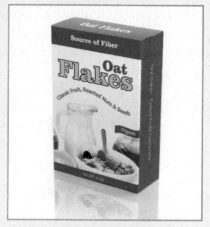

Containers with a large surface area also allow the manufacturer to better advertise their product.

Height (cm)	Length (cm)	Width (cm)	Volume (cm³)	Surface Area (SA) (cm²)	Volume to SA (ratio)
25.5	20.0	6.6	3,366	1,621	
27.0	19.0	6.7	3,437	1,642	
26.5	19.0	6.8	3,424	1,626	
26.0	19.0	6.9	3,409	1,609	
25.5	19.0	7.0	3,392	1,592	
27.0	18.0	7.1	3,451	1,611	
26.5	18.0	7.2	3,434	1,595	
26.0	18.0	7.3	3,416	1,578	
25.5	18.0	7.4	3,397	1,562	

5. For each set of box dimensions, determine the volume-to-surface-area ratio. Round the results to two decimal places. Choose the box that best meets the criteria and explain your reasoning.

EVIDENCE NOTEBOOK

6. Why do design engineers test promising solutions to a problem, such as preventing plates from breaking, before finalizing the design? Record your evidence.

Identify the Characteristics of the Best Solution

One design may not perform the best across all tests, so identifying the best-performing characteristics of the designs can help design the best solution to the problem. This is an important step in optimizing solutions.

A raincoat designer wants to make raincoats that teenagers would like. The company's engineers tested three different designs that performed well in three different tests. However, no design performed the best in all the tests. The design criteria are identified as follows:

- It must be as lightweight as possible.
- It must to be easy to close and open.
- It must be as water resistant as possible.
- It must be made of fabrics with fashionable designs and colors.
- It must have pockets.

Optimizing a raincoat design involves working with a design that combines the most favorable characteristics.

	Weight (g)	Closure	Fabric Water Resistance (minutes of exposure)
Raincoat A	250	Snaps: hard to use	11
Raincoat B	410	Zipper: easy to use	27
Raincoat C	500	Zipper: easy to use	>60

The three criteria identified as the most important for a successful design were: being lightweight, being easy to close, and having high water resistance. Engineers made a new design that combined the best features of each raincoat. This redesign had the weight range of Raincoat A, the water-resistant fabric of Raincoat C, and the zipper of Raincoats B and C. The redesigned raincoat was then tested. Tests showed that the most water-resistant fabric worked in the new design, but it was a little heavier because of the heavier fabric.

7. Imagine you are in charge of further optimizing the raincoat design. What next steps would you take in the optimization process?

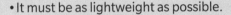

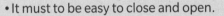

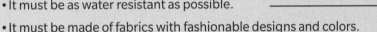

Using Data to Optimize Solutions

Some engineering problems involve designing a process or system rather than designing an object. The assembly line is an example of a system that has become an important manufacturing system. In an automotive assembly line, a car's frame moves on an automated belt system. As the cars or its parts move by, each worker along the line performs a specific task. At the end of the assembly line is a finished car. The assembly line is process-designed to solve an engineering problem—making many similar or identical objects as efficiently as possible. Assembly lines are used to produce many things, such as clothing, tools, food, and vehicles. Engineers whose job it is to optimize industrial systems are called *industrial engineers*.

Process and System Optimization

Engineered systems are designed to solve a well-defined problem. Although assembly line systems were used during the Industrial Revolution to speed up the manufacturing process, it was not until the early 20th century that they were optimized to include the types of processes that are used today.

Henry Ford and his team designed the first modern assembly line to produce large numbers of cars. Each major car part was produced on a separate line. Then a final line assembled the vehicle. Every worker carried out a specific task. The time needed to build a single car dropped from 12 hours to about 90 minutes. Optimizing assembly lines allowed Ford's main factory to increase production from fewer than 20,000 cars a year to more than a million cars per year in just 10 years. Ford was able to reduce the price of his cars by reducing the time, cost, and number of people it took to build them.

The assembly line has changed through continual optimization. Today, assembly lines are often made up of rows of robots doing repetitive tasks for long periods of time instead of rows of human workers doing the same thing.

8. The assembly line has changed over time. How is the optimization of engineered processes similar to the optimization of engineered products?

The Iterative Design Process

Part of design optimization includes iterative testing of a prototype. The results of iterative tests are used to improve the next design version. For example, suppose a company that makes bicycle parts is designing a new gear sprocket. Bicycle sprockets are most often made from an alloy of aluminum and zinc. The alloy is light and is available in a variety of strengths. The sprocket design works well, but designers now want to make it from the strongest alloy they can. To identify the most suitable alloy, designers will test the sprocket design using different alloys. Strength tests will identify the strongest alloy. The sprocket design will be modified to use the new, stronger alloy.

Several sprockets make up the gears of a bicycle.

The Systematic Steps of Optimizing a Design Solution

This diagram represents the "ideal" engineering design process. In reality, engineers may skip steps or do things in different orders. Iterative design processes are used to optimize the solution. The optimizing steps are highlighted.

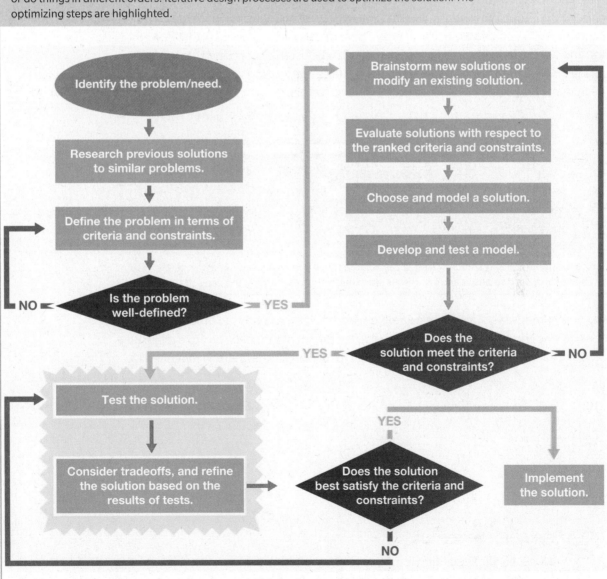

9. What are some characteristics of the iterative design process? Choose all that apply.

    A. Each iteration incorporates features that worked in previous tests.

    B. Useful features of different solutions can be combined.

    C. Solutions are tested during every iteration of the design process.

    D. Each iteration starts with a completely new idea or solution.

The Space Pen

An example of a product of the iterative design process is the "space pen," a ballpoint pen that can work in zero gravity. Astronauts on early space missions used pencils to keep notes, but using pencils created problems. Broken tips and graphite dust floated around the cabin and interfered with instruments. The developer of the space pen, Paul Fisher, used the iterative process to optimize the design solution for writing in space. In the freefall conditions of space, the ink in a regular pen dried out or it did not flow in the right direction. Fisher designed a cartridge to hold the ink. However, a vacuum formed in the cartridge, and the ink stopped flowing. To solve this problem, he pressurized the ink cartridge. Then the ink flowed well. However, sometimes it leaked because of the air pressure. To improve the performance, Fisher developed a gel-like ink that flowed well and did not leak. The result was a pen that can be used in space and that can write upside down on Earth. In each iteration, the features that worked were improved, and the features that did not work were not developed further.

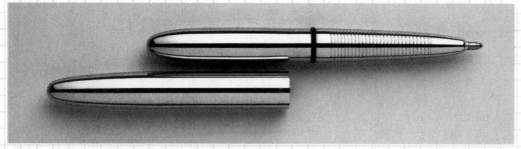

During the iterative design process used to develop the space pen, many solutions were tested. Each iteration of proposed solutions and test results led to more improvements in the pen's design.

10. Sometimes the solution for one problem leads to new solutions to other problems. Use evidence from the example of the development of the space pen to explain how the problem of developing a ballpoint pen for use on Earth was likely redefined.

EVIDENCE NOTEBOOK

    11. Even after a solution is used, engineers often return to the original problem and work to refine the solution. How is the iterative design process helpful in developing a solution to breaking plates? Record your evidence.

Hands-On Lab
Design a Model Car, Part 3

Evaluate test data and optimize a design.

In Part 2 of this lab, you built your model car. Now, in Part 3, you and other groups in your class will evaluate and optimize your car designs. The exact steps of your optimization process can vary depending on the number of cars built and the time available. Refer to the instructions in Part 1 of this lab (in Lesson 2) for the criteria and constraints for the car designs and the materials list.

MATERIALS
- See materials from Design a Model Car, Part 1.

Procedure and Analysis

STEP 1 Compare your test results from Part 2 of this lab with the results of other groups who tested the same design variables. Describe how those variables are related to the distance traveled.

STEP 2 Are there characteristics of other groups' cars that performed better in the tests than your car's? Based on your comparison of the class results, propose three design changes that could improve your car's performance, if needed. List your proposed design changes. Identify how you think the proposed design change will improve the car's performance. If you believe your car design does not need improvement, explain your reasoning.

STEP 3 With your teacher's approval, apply one design change to your car. Repeat the test and record your data on a separate sheet of paper. Compare the data from your modified design to the data from your original design.

STEP 4 How did the design change affect performance?

STEP 5 As a class, discuss and evaluate all of the test results and make suggestions for a new iteration of the design that uses the best characteristics of each design.

STEP 6 Each component of the solution must relate to the problem as it is defined. For example, unless the clearance between the car body and the ground meets specifications for the ramp the cars will roll down, the car might get stuck as it leaves the ramp. How do the car's wheels relate to the car as a solution to the engineering problem?

STEP 7 How might taking the best-performing characteristics of different car designs and using them to redesign your car help improve it?

Combine the Best Parts of Solutions

After a product is introduced, the iterative process continues, often leading to development of new models or styles. Each new style is a solution to a restated design problem that is influenced by successes and failures of the previous solutions. For example, cell phones have changed over time, as shown in the photo. Touchscreens have replaced keypads, and antennas are now contained within the phone. Optimization of the phone's built-in camera has added a major new function to cell phones. Point-and-shoot cameras, once popular devices, have been almost entirely replaced by cell phones.

During the optimization of cell phones, tradeoffs were necessary.

12. Improvements to one function frequently lead to worse performance of another function. Which of these statements describes a tradeoff that was needed as cell phones changed to meet new criteria and constraints? Choose all that apply.

A. Larger cell phone screens allow new functions, such as viewing videos.

B. Adding more applications shortens the life of a battery.

C. Bigger screens have a larger glass surface area, making them easier to shatter.

D. Internal antennas increase portability but decrease signal reception.

E. Touchscreens increase viewing area but can be harder to use than buttons.

F. Thinner cases decrease the weight of the phone and make it easier to handle.

13. How might starting the engineering design process with only one idea affect the ability to optimize that design later on?

_____

_____

_____

_____

_____

Continue Your Exploration

Name: _____   Date: _____

Check out the path below or go online to choose one of the other paths shown.

People in Engineering

- Rapid Prototyping (3D Printers)
- Hands-On Labs 🖐
- Propose Your Own Path

Go online to choose one of these other paths.

Ellen Ochoa, Electrical Engineer

Ellen Ochoa is an astronaut who became the director of the Johnson Space Center in Houston, Texas, in 2013. As a student working on her doctorate in electrical engineering, and later as a researcher at NASA, she designed optical data systems for processing information using light signals. She became an astronaut in 1991 and flew on four Space Shuttle missions. Her jobs included developing software and computer hardware for space flights and robotics development and testing. Besides being an astronaut, a manager, and a research engineer, Ochoa is a classical flutist.

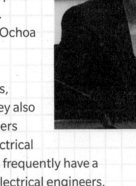

Electrical engineers design, develop, and test electrical equipment, such as electric motors, radar and navigation systems, communications systems, and power-generation equipment. They also supervise the manufacturing of this equipment. Electrical engineers who work in industrial careers often have bachelor's degrees. Electrical engineers who direct research at university and government labs frequently have a doctorate. As Ellen Ochoa has shown, the sky is not the limit for electrical engineers.

Ellen Ochoa became the first Hispanic woman to go to space when she served as a mission specialist aboard the Space Shuttle Discovery in 1993.

Continue Your Exploration

1. List three industries that would likely employ electrical engineers. Then describe one job that would likely involve electrical engineering in each industry.

2. Why might a person who is thinking about studying electrical engineering need to think about whether they enjoy solving problems?

3. Ellen Ochoa was accepted by NASA as an astronaut after she established her career as an electrical engineer. Why would a career in electrical engineering be a useful background for an astronaut?

4. **Collaborate** Research one or more electrical engineers who are involved in research. On a sheet of paper, generate a list of questions to ask the engineers about their work. With your teacher's help, contact one or more of these engineers to interview. Present your findings to the class.

Can You Explain It?

Name: _____   Date: _____

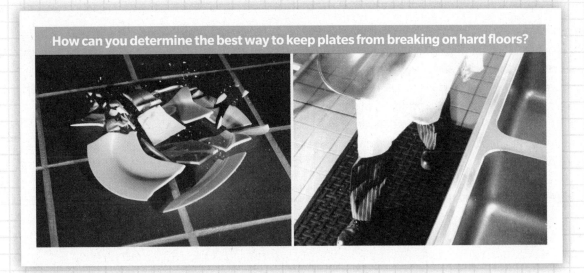

How can you determine the best way to keep plates from breaking on hard floors?

EVIDENCE NOTEBOOK

Refer to the notes in your Evidence Notebook to help you describe how to optimize a solution to the problem of plates breaking on floors.

1. State your claim. Make sure your reasoning fully explains how a solution may be optimized to solve the problem.

2. Summarize the evidence you have gathered to support your claim and explain your reasoning.

Checkpoints

Answer the following questions to check your understanding of the lesson.

Use the data in the table to answer Questions 3–5.

3. Your team is building a rocket to enter into a national competition. Scoring is based on three factors: how high the rocket flies, time of flight before the parachute opens, and how safely it delivers a cargo of three eggs. Safely delivering all three eggs is a constraint. You test four different design solutions and record the results, which are averaged here. Which designs could be acceptable within the constraint? Select all that apply.

	Height (m)	Time of flight (s)	Number of eggs unbroken
Rocket A	260	49	3
Rocket B	220	57	1
Rocket C	240	66	3
Rocket D	275	58	2

   A. Rocket A   C. Rocket C

   B. Rocket B   D. Rocket D

4. The iterative process involves testing the *most promising / rejected* solutions and modifying the *size / design* based on test results. Iterative testing can be carried out to *prototype / optimize* the most successful design.

5. You want to improve the height your rocket can reach. Which of the following features should you use in your new design?

   A. the dimensions of Rocket A

   B. the dimensions of Rocket B

   C. the dimensions of Rocket C

   D. the dimensions of Rocket D

Use the photo to answer Question 6.

6. This engineer is testing scale models of bridge components. Why might he use scale models in his tests rather than full-scale models? Choose all that apply.

   A. Scale models are less expensive to construct than actual pillars.

   B. Using models allows the engineer to test many different combinations of materials.

   C. The engineer will be able to find the best combination of materials for the bridge.

   D. Models are able to exactly reproduce the function of a pillar, but the testing is faster.

Interactive Review

Complete this section to review the main concepts of the lesson.

The solution that best addresses the ranked criteria of the engineering problem is chosen to further refine.

A. Why is it important to compare test results when making decisions about what design to develop further?

The iterative design process is a tool that engineers use to build the best solution. It is used to identify ways a solution can be improved further to better address the criteria and constraints of the design problem.

B. After a solution has been built, why might engineers want to optimize it further? What design process would they likely use to optimize a solution?

Choose one of the activities below to explore how this unit connects to other topics.

People in Science

Luis von Ahn, Computer Scientist Luis von Ahn researches problems that can be solved by many people working together, an area he calls *human computation*. Von Ahn grew up in Guatemala City and became interested in computers at a young age. He earned degrees in math and computer science. His work on Internet security tests and the digitizing of data shows that humans and computers can work together to solve complex problems.

Present a human-computation project to your class. Explain the project goal, the roles of humans and computers in the project, and why its goals are possible only through human-computer collaboration.

Social Studies Connection

Epic Failures Many inventors and scientists "failed" before making a big discovery. The Wright brothers became successful only after experimenting with hundreds of glider flights and airplane designs.

Conduct research and make a verbal presentation about another person in history who persevered through adversity before having his or her invention succeed. Describe how the inventor refined the device using the engineering design process.

Life Science Connection

Biomedicine Medical biology, or biomedicine, is the application of biological research to medical practices. This field of study includes specialties ranging from laboratory diagnostics to vaccine development and gene therapy. Engineers in the field of biomedicine work to design biomedical devices and develop biotechnologies.

Research a biomedical invention, therapy, or process and the history of its development. Prepare a multimedia presentation describing how the engineering design process contributed to the development of a successful treatment solution.

Name: _____   Date: _____

Complete this review to check your understanding of the unit.

Use the diagram to answer Questions 1–3.

1. This diagram is an example of information flowing through a system. What is an example of this system's output?

    A. brainstorming solutions

    B. a successful solution

    C. evaluation of potential solutions

    D. evaluation of test data

2. Which step in the engineering design process comes immediately after brainstorming solutions?

    A. describing the problem

    B. evaluating solutions with respect to criteria

    C. choosing solutions for testing

    D. any of the above

3. Testing and evaluating solutions is a(n) *iterative / linear* process.

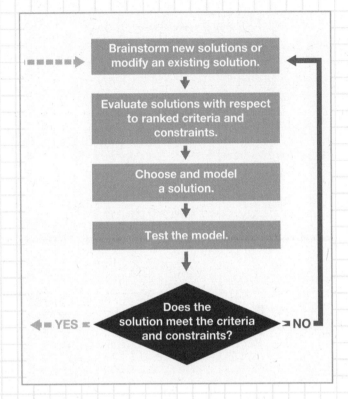

Use the decision matrix to answer Questions 4–5.

Decision Matrix: The Best Screen Protector			
Criteria	**Materials**		
	TPU	Tempered glass	PET film
Does not scratch	2	4	4
Reduces glare	2	3	2
Lightweight	2	2	1
Durable	1	4	4
Not expensive	3	1	2

4. This decision matrix ranks screen protector materials according to several specifications. Which material would make the best screen protector if the most important features were *Not expensive* and *Reduces glare*?

    A. TPU (thermoplastic polyurethane)

    B. Tempered glass

    C. PET film (polyethylene terephthalate)

5. The materials are the *criteria / solutions* in the decision matrix. The specifications about each option are the *criteria / solutions* .

6. Think about the engineering design process as you fill out this chart. Describe how each of the steps involves aspects of each of the big-picture concepts.

Process Steps	Criteria and Constraints	Research and Data Analysis	Systems and System Models
Defining an engineering problem	Determining the most important criteria and constraints helps to precisely define the design problem by identifying specific needs and limitations.		
Testing a solution			
Making tradeoffs			

Name: _____   Date: _____

Use the photo of the mind-controlled prosthetic arm to answer Questions 7–10.

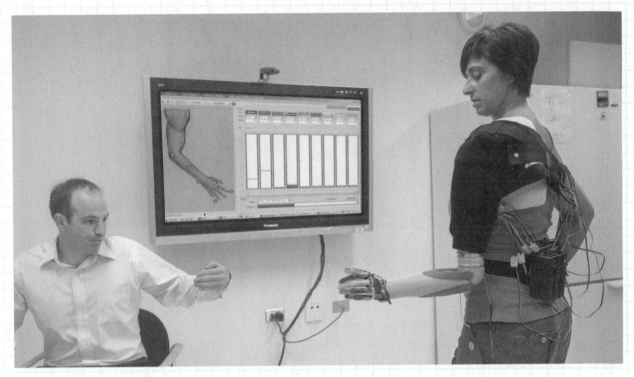

7. The photo shows a woman controlling the movements of her prosthetic arm using brain signals. Describe the problem that this tool solves.

8. People using this new type of prosthetic have noticed that some of their needs are not met by the current design. Based on these comments, the engineers are working to address these issues and are developing a new prototype. Explain why a new prototype is necessary.

9. What criteria do you think the inventors determined were important when developing their prototype?

10. What scientific principles might have guided the inventors of this prosthetic arm?

Use the photos to answer Questions 11–14.

11. What needs does each suitcase address? Are they the same needs? Explain your answer.

12. What kinds of data could you collect about suitcase designs to compare the needs each different style meets? What tests would be the most helpful in comparing how each design solution solves a problem or need?

13. After analyzing the data from suitcase design tests, you may find that both options have good features. Explain how engineers might use these results to develop an improved solution.

14. Suitcase designs have changed over time. Use evidence to explain how suitcase design has benefited from the engineering design process.

Name: _____ Date: _____

What is the best feature for a new pool entry ramp?

An inspector has determined that the entrance ramp for your community pool does not meet current safety requirements. The pool management board is looking at ways to upgrade the current ramp to meet the standards. They are looking at reducing the slope of the ramp, coating the ramp with non-slip surface material, and/or installing railings.

Your team has been asked to analyze design solutions to determine which ramp modification is the most appropriate and affordable choice for your community pool. You will present your findings to the pool directors as they decide how to proceed.

The steps below will help guide your research and develop your recommendation.

Engineer It

1. **Define the Problem** Define the design problem using the criteria and constraints. How might each type of ramp modification increase safety for different types of pool patrons?

Engineer It

2. **Conduct Research** Consider each of the three pool ramp feature options (changing the ramp angle, the surface material, and/or the railings). Explain what types of work would have to be done in order to make that type of ramp modification. How might each of these changes help the pool meet current safety rules?

3. **Analyze Data** On a separate sheet of paper, create a decision matrix to analyze the modification options. Describe the strengths and weaknesses of each modification option.

4. **Identify and Recommend a Solution** Based on your research, construct a written explanation about which pool ramp feature change is the best choice for your community pool. Describe any tradeoffs involved in your decision.

5. **Communicate** Prepare a presentation of your recommendation for the community pool directors as they decide which design is best for the ramp. Include an argument for your recommendation based on evidence and an explanation of the benefits and drawbacks associated with the design.

 Self-Check

	I precisely defined the criteria and constraints that helped define the problem of improving pool ramp safety.
	I researched the design features to determine how well they met the criteria and constraints of the problem.
	I analyzed my research and data to create a decision matrix.
	My solution is based on evidence from research, and an analysis of my decision matrix.
	My solution and recommendation were clearly communicated to others.

Systems in Organisms and Earth

How do interactions among natural systems make life on Earth possible?

Rock climbing requires a combination of muscle strength, balance, and hand-eye coordination.

You Solve It How Can You Design a Satellite's Orbit?

Design and test orbits for two satellites that will be put into orbit around the Earth and Mars systems.

Go online and complete the You Solve It to explore ways to solve a real-world problem.

Investigate an Animal Behavior

Dolphins identify the size and position of prey using sound waves.

A. Look at the photo of the dolphin. On a separate sheet of paper, write down as many different questions as you can about the photo.

B. Discuss With your class or a partner, share your questions. Record any additional questions generated in your discussion. Then, choose the most important questions from the list that are related to animal behavior. Write them below.

C. Identify an animal that has an interesting behavior that you would like to research. List some of the sources you might use in your research.

D. Use the information above and your research to produce a multimedia presentation or science magazine article describing the animal's behavior. Include body and sensory adaptations involved in the behavior.

Discuss the next steps for your Unit Project with your teacher and go online to download the Unit Project Worksheet.

Language Development

Use the lessons in this unit to complete the network and expand your understanding of these key concepts.

Similar term
Phrase
Cognate
Example
Definition

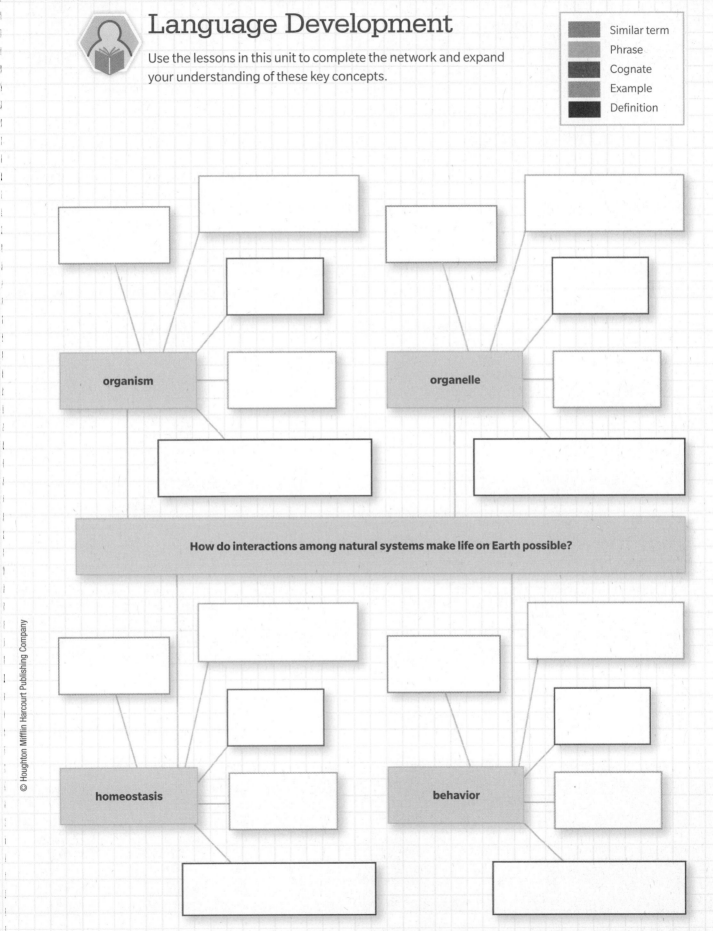

organism

organelle

How do interactions among natural systems make life on Earth possible?

homeostasis

behavior

Models Help Scientists Study Natural Systems

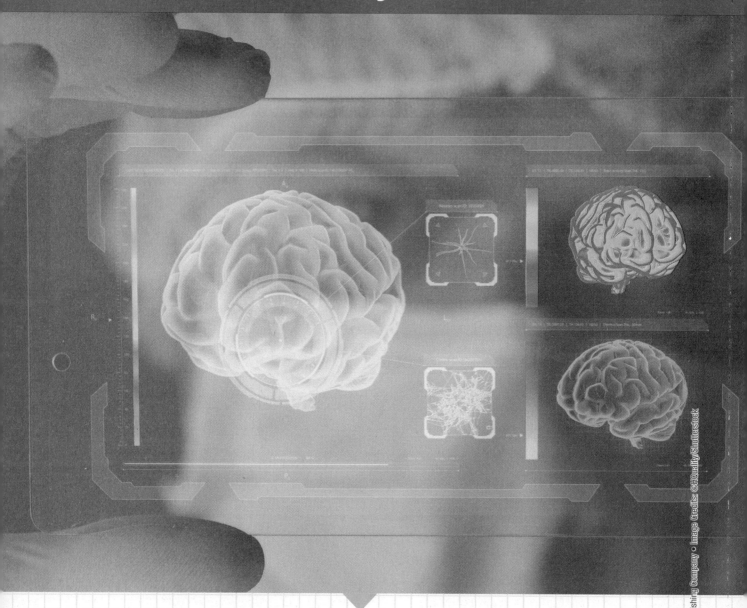

This digital holographic plate combines an image projection and a mathematical model to visualize the different parts of the brain.

Explore First

Evaluating Models Analyze a drawing of a brain, a computer-generated image of a flower, or a map that shows the location of water in your area. In what ways does the model help you understand the system it represents? In what ways is the model limited? Record the pros and cons of the model in a table.

Go online to view the digital version of the Hands-On Lab for this lesson and to download additional lab resources.

CAN YOU EXPLAIN IT?

How can this model help scientists study natural systems?

Biosphere 2 was built to determine if a physical model of the Earth system could sustain life. Today, the facility is an education and research center.

Biosphere 2 was designed to support a small team of researchers for two years, completely sealed off from the outside environment. It contained thousands of species of plants and animals in different environments, including an ocean with a coral reef. However, low oxygen and high carbon dioxide levels resulted in many problems and endangered the lives of the researchers. Although the project did not achieve its goals, scientists gained an understanding of how systems on Earth interact.

1. **Discuss** Study the photo that shows Biosphere 2 from the outside. What do you think it would be like to live inside for two years?

2. Why might scientists and engineers want to find out if a system like Biosphere 2 can sustain life?

 EVIDENCE NOTEBOOK As you explore the lesson, gather information to help explain how the Biosphere 2 model helps scientists study natural systems.

Defining Systems

What do you think of when you hear the word, "system"? You might think of a video game system, the solar system, or your digestive system. Scientists define and study systems to help them construct explanations and make predictions. For example, scientists study coral reef systems to explain interactions between organisms and to analyze the effects of human activities on the environment.

3. There is no hard boundary between a coral reef and the open ocean. How does defining a boundary help scientists to better study a coral reef? Select all that apply.

   A. Defining a coral reef boundary allows scientists to explain all ocean parts and interactions by studying the reef as a system.

   B. Defining a coral reef boundary allows scientists to focus on a smaller set of parts and interactions.

   C. Defining a coral reef boundary allows scientists to see how the parts of the reef interact with the parts of the rest of the ocean.

   D. Defining a coral reef boundary allows scientists to decide that the reef is not part of the ocean.

Coral skeletons form the reef structure that many animals, including fishes, urchins, and crabs, rely on for food and shelter.

Explore Online

Systems

A **system** is a set of interacting parts working together. Corals, fishes, and seawater are all parts, or *components*, of a coral reef system. Organisms in the system interact with each other, their environment, and components of other systems. One organism can be food or shelter for other organisms. For example, algae growing on reefs use energy from sunlight to make food by photosynthesis. Parrotfish eat the algae and hide from predators in the reef openings. Sharks visit the reef to prey on parrotfish and other animals. All of these interactions result in transfers of matter and energy.

Matter and energy flow into, within, or out of systems. Matter or energy that enters a system is called an *input*. A coral reef system relies on inputs of seawater and sunlight. Some inputs harm reefs. Pollution from industry or runoff is an example of a harmful input. A product of a system is an *output*. The output of one part of the system can become the input for another part. For example, algae and other producers release oxygen during the process of photosynthesis. Organisms in the coral reef system use the oxygen in the process of cellular respiration.

Natural Systems

A coral reef is a *natural system,* because it occurs in the natural world and was not designed by people. Scientists are interested in understanding how natural systems function and change while engineers are interested in studying and solving problems. For example, scientists might study a coral reef system to determine how pollution affects coral reef health. Engineers might develop a computer model to identify the source of the pollution and design and test affordable methods to reduce or stop the pollution.

In order to study a system, a scientist starts by imagining a *boundary,* or surface that encloses the system. In a natural system, like a coral reef, matter and energy pass into and out of the boundary. When fish, crabs, and bits of drifting seaweed flow through the imaginary boundary, they become components of the reef ecosystem.

Natural systems have *properties*, or characteristics, that result from the interactions of their parts. For example, temperature and salinity are properties of a coral reef system.

4. Discuss Your body is another example of a natural system. Brainstorm parts of your body system and record them to complete the model below.

Boundary

Inputs/Outputs

oxygen

Components

organs

Interactions

breathing

Properties

personality

 EVIDENCE NOTEBOOK

5. What is the boundary of the Biosphere 2 system? How is this boundary similar to a natural system? How is it different? Record your evidence.

Modeling Systems

Scientists and engineers use models to represent natural systems. When scientists and engineers construct models of systems, they include only the parts and interactions that are most important for their intended purpose. Then they can improve the model by comparing it with the real system. For example, the diagram on this page is a conceptual model intended to communicate the parts of the human respiratory system. It shows some of the system features, but does not include details at the microscopic scale.

Models can be physical, mathematical, digital, or conceptual, or combinations of these different model types.

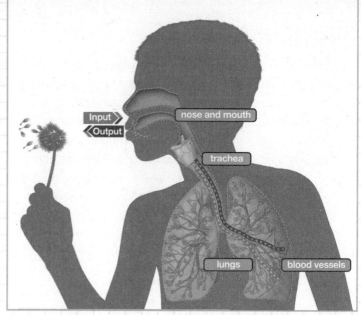

This diagram is a conceptual model of the respiratory system.

Define a System

Think of something that you could define as a system to help you study how it works. It could be your classroom, favorite animal, or sports team. List the features of your system including the boundary, inputs and outputs, components, and interactions.

6. Record your system and system features in the graphic organizer.

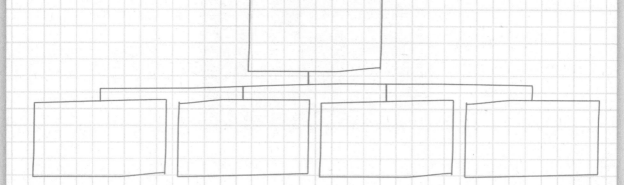

7. Summarize the evidence you collected to define your system.

Modeling Living Systems

Organisms Are Living Systems

A bacterium, a tree, and a rat are all living things, yet they look very different and perform different activities. However, all living things, or organisms, perform basic life functions. An **organism** is a living system made up of one or more cells that perform all the functions needed for life and growth. The body of a complex organism can be organized into subsystems that interact to perform functions. For example, your body has a circulatory system and a respiratory system that work together to deliver oxygen and nutrients to all the cells in your body.

Cells

All organisms are made of cells. A **cell** is the smallest subsystem of an organism that can perform all the functions needed for life. Organisms that are made up of a single cell are called *unicellular* organisms. *Multicellular* organisms are made of more than one cell. The cell types that make up multicellular organisms are specialized and organized to carry out specific functions.

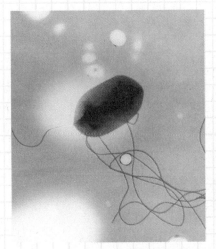

E. coli bacteria are unicellular. They have whip-like structures that help them move and attach to host cells.

Ponderosa pine trees are multicellular plants. They have a thick outer layer, or *bark*, that protects them from the sun.

The kangaroo rat is a multicellular animal. Its specialized body system allows it to survive with very little water.

8. Each cell in unicellular organisms performs some/all of the functions required for life. Each cell in a multicellular organism performs some/all of the functions required for life.

Tissues

In organisms, such as plants and animals, specialized cells are grouped together in tissues. A **tissue** is a subsystem made up of a group of similar cells that are organized to perform a specific function. For example, certain specialized cells in a plant are small and hollow. These cells connect together to form a tissue, called *vascular tissue*, that transports water throughout the plant.

Hands-On Lab
Model Tissue Structure and Function

You will model two different tissue types and relate their structure to their function.

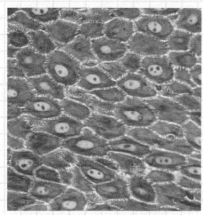

This tissue protects the skin from scraping. It can be especially thick on the heels of your feet.

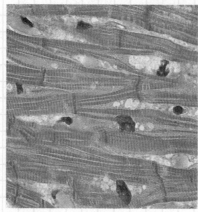

This tissue is located in the heart. It stretches and contracts to make the heart pump blood.

MATERIALS
- adhesive putty
- beads
- cardboard
- construction paper
- foam peanuts
- glue
- markers
- modeling clay
- pom poms
- rice
- rubber bands
- scissors
- sponges
- tape

Procedure and Analysis

STEP 1 Look at the tissues in the photos. Record your observations about the structure and shape of the cells.

STEP 2 Select the materials that you think will best model the cells and how they are connected to form the tissues. Construct a model of each tissue.

STEP 3 Describe how your models represent groups of cells working together to form tissues.

STEP 4 Use your models to make a claim about how the role played by different types of tissues within an organ depends on the structure of its cells.

Organs

An **organ** is a subsystem made up of different tissue types that work together to perform a function. For example, the stem of a plant is an organ that is made up of vascular tissue that transports water and nutrients, ground tissue that provides support, and epidermal tissue that protects the outside of the stem. Blood vessels are organs in animals made up of epithelial tissue that controls the passage of blood cells, layers of smooth muscle tissue that control the diameter of the vessel, and a tough wall of connective tissue.

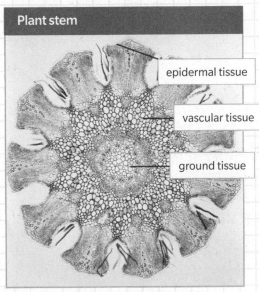

Plant stem

- epidermal tissue
- vascular tissue
- ground tissue

Stems are plant organs that transport materials and provide support for the plant.

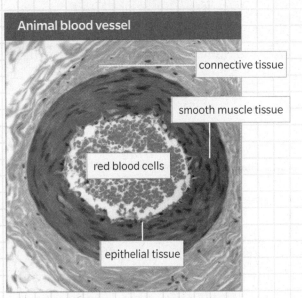

Animal blood vessel

- connective tissue
- smooth muscle tissue
- red blood cells
- epithelial tissue

Blood vessels transport blood and nutrients and remove wastes in the body.

Organ Systems

An **organ system** is a subsystem made up of a group of organs that work together to perform body functions. For example, in animals the heart, lungs, and blood vessels are organs of the *circulatory system* that takes in oxygen from the air through the process of respiration and delivers it to all the cells in the body. In plants, the leaves, stems, and flowers are organs of the *shoot system*, which transports water and nutrients from the roots to the leaves and uses carbon dioxide from the air and sunlight to produce food through the process of photosynthesis. An organism can have many organ systems that work together to perform all the functions the organism needs to survive.

9. Draw a model that shows the relationship between cells, tissues, organs, and organ systems.

10. When this frilled lizard is threatened, its heart rate increases to prepare to fight or run. Label the subsystems to complete the lizard circulatory system infographic.

organ system

This subsystem is specialized for contraction. The structure of protein fibers inside allows it to stretch and contract.

Special junctions where cells connect allow all the cells in this subsystem to contract at the same time.

Several tissue types work together in this heart to perform the function of pumping blood throughout the body system.

Language SmArts

Use Evidence to Support an Argument

11. Use evidence from the text and the lizard diagram to support an argument that living things are made up of subsystems that can be part of larger systems.

_____

_____

_____

_____

_____

_____

_____

Modeling Earth Systems

Earth Is a System

The boundary of the Earth system surrounds the entire planet, including the atmosphere. The system includes all the matter, energy, and processes within this boundary. The Earth system includes nonliving things, such as water, rocks, and air. It also includes living things, such as trees, animals, and people.

The Earth system is made up of smaller subsystems that constantly interact as matter and energy cycle and flow among them. The transfer of energy from the sun and Earth's interior drive the transfer of matter among the subsystems. Energy can also be transferred by the action of waves and moving objects. These interactions can happen in just a fraction of a second or over billions of years.

The Earth system can be divided into four major subsystems: the geosphere, the hydrosphere, the atmosphere, and the biosphere.

12. Identify the components of each subsystem as living or nonliving things.

biosphere _____   atmosphere _____

hydrosphere _____   geosphere _____

13. Discuss Brainstorm ways in which the components of the different subsystems interact with each other.

Geosphere

Nearly all the mass of Earth is in the *geosphere*, the Earth subsystem that includes all rocks, minerals, and landforms on Earth's surface and all the matter in Earth's interior.

The geosphere is constantly changing. Thermal energy from Earth's formation and the decay of radioactive rocks drive changes on the surface that we experience as earthquakes, volcanoes, and the gradual buildup of mountains. Erosion by wind and water wears away landforms, and shapes rivers, lakes, and canyons.

These *tufa* pinnacles formed underwater 10,000 to 100,000 years ago.

Hydrosphere and Cryosphere

The *hydrosphere* is all the water on Earth. Ninety-seven percent of the hydrosphere is salt water found in the oceans. The hydrosphere also includes the fresh water in lakes, rivers, and underground. Rain and water droplets in clouds are also part of the hydrosphere. The *cryosphere* is a subsystem of the hydrosphere, made up of all the frozen water on Earth, such as glaciers, sea ice, and the snow shown in the photo.

Water on Earth is constantly moving as it flows through rivers, rocks, and living things. Energy from the sun drives the water cycle, which circulates water between Earth's surface and the atmosphere.

Liquid and frozen water are present at Lake Tahoe during the winter months.

Atmosphere

The *atmosphere* is the mixture of gases and particles that surround Earth. Nitrogen makes up about 78% of the atmosphere. Oxygen makes up nearly 21% of the atmosphere. The remaining 1% includes carbon dioxide, water vapor, and trace amounts of other gases. The atmosphere absorbs some of the energy from the sun. This energy warms Earth and makes life possible. Earth's rotation and uneven warming by the sun result in winds and air currents that move air and thermal energy around Earth.

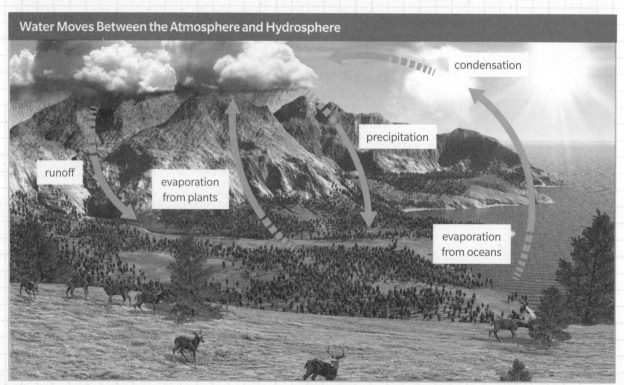

Water Moves Between the Atmosphere and Hydrosphere

condensation

precipitation

runoff

evaporation from plants

evaporation from oceans

© Houghton Mifflin Harcourt Publishing Company • Image Credits: (t) ©Sierralara/RooM/ Getty Images; (m) ©Anton Foltin/Shutterstock;

14. The diagram shows some of the interactions between the atmosphere and the hydrosphere. Identify the inputs and outputs of each system. Use your observations to explain how the inputs of one subsystem can be outputs of another subsystem.

Biosphere

The biosphere is made up of living things, including all the plants, animals, and microorganisms found everywhere on Earth. The biosphere extends upward about ten kilometers, and down to the deepest ocean trenches. Living things depend on other living things and nonliving things in their environment to exist.

   The sun is the source of energy for green plants and other organisms that produce food using photosynthesis. Almost all life depends on these producers, since animals and most other organisms cannot make their own food. Animals and other consumers get food by eating plants or other organisms. Matter and energy move through the biosphere and other Earth subsystems as living things eat, grow, breathe, and move.

15. Wildfires occur naturally or are caused by human negligence. They spread quickly and emit harmful carbon particles into the air. Describe the ways a wildfire can affect the biosphere.

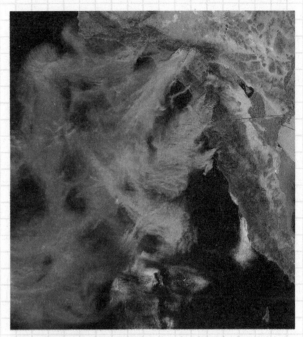

This satellite image shows the clouds of smoke from massive wildfires moving over the ocean.

16. *Decomposition* occurs when bacteria, fungi, or worms in the soil break down the matter in an organism that has died. Decomposition transfers matter from the geosphere / biosphere to the geosphere / biosphere.

EVIDENCE NOTEBOOK

   17. All of Earth's subsystems are represented in Biosphere 2. How can this help scientists understand interactions between subsystems? Record your evidence.

© Houghton Mifflin Harcourt Publishing Company • Image Credits: ©Jacques Descloitres/MODIS Rapid Response Team/NASA Goddard Space Flight Center

Anthroposphere

A recently recognized Earth subsystem is the anthroposphere. The *anthroposphere* includes the total human presence on Earth, including built structures, technologies, activities, economy, and culture.

The anthroposphere is greatly affecting other Earth subsystems at a rapid rate. Human activities are changing carbon dioxide levels in the atmosphere and the amount of sea ice in the cryosphere. Human populations and the use of natural resources place stresses on the biosphere and geosphere.

Human-built cities are part of the anthroposphere.

18. List the Earth subsystem most affected by the activity described.

clear-cutting rainforest to make way for a railroad	
burning gasoline in cars	
draining wetlands to make space to build housing	
mining for coal and minerals	

Model Agricultural Runoff

Agricultural runoff occurs when water moves from farms to other areas due to rain, melting snow, or irrigation. Runoff collects the added nutrients from farm fields and carries them to lakes, coastlines, and groundwater.

If farms are not managed well, nutrient pollution is a problem. Manure and fertilizers high in nitrogen and phosphorus affect water quality.

19. **Draw** and label a model showing how the products of agricultural runoff travel through the Earth's subsystems. Indicate the transfer of matter between the subsystems, impacting fish and other living things.

Using Models to Analyze Systems

Studying Natural Systems Using Models

Natural events and human activities can result in changes to living and Earth systems over time. These changes can occur rapidly or very slowly over millions of years. Scientists use models to monitor changes that are occurring and to predict changes that might occur in the future. Scientists can compare predictions of their models with changes in the real world to refine their models so they will be more accurate.

Case Study: Modeling Changes to Coral Reefs

Coral reef systems are changing in response to human activities. Carbon emissions into the atmosphere result in increased global air and water temperatures. Algae that live in the tissues of coral provide food to the corals and are also responsible for the coral color. High temperatures stress the coral and cause them to release their algae partners. This appears as "bleaching", or lack of color, and eventually leads to coral death.

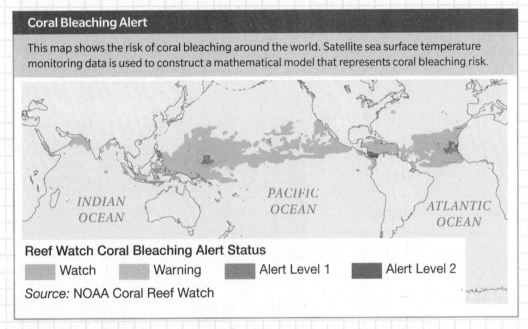

Coral Bleaching Alert

This map shows the risk of coral bleaching around the world. Satellite sea surface temperature monitoring data is used to construct a mathematical model that represents coral bleaching risk.

INDIAN OCEAN

PACIFIC OCEAN

ATLANTIC OCEAN

Reef Watch Coral Bleaching Alert Status

Watch   Warning   Alert Level 1   Alert Level 2

Source: NOAA Coral Reef Watch

20. **Discuss** How can scientists use this model to better understand how climate change affects interactions in coral reef systems?

EVIDENCE NOTEBOOK

21. How could Biosphere 2 be used to make predictions about the effects of climate change on natural systems? Record your evidence.

22. Do the Math What is the projected temperature increase by 2099 if carbon emissions are not reduced? What is the projection if carbon emissions are reduced?

23. Carbon emissions in the atmosphere can enter the hydrosphere and cause acidification of ocean water, which can negatively affect the health of coral reefs. What can scientists infer about the future health of coral reef systems based on this climate change model?

Carbon Emissions and Temperature Increase

This model shows the relationship between carbon emissions in the atmosphere due to human activities and the projected increase in global temperature over time.

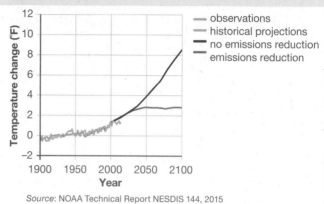

Source: NOAA Technical Report NESDIS 144, 2015

24. Discuss How can conservation scientists use the bleaching risk and climate change models to improve strategies for protecting coral reef ecosystems?

Engineer It

Evaluate a Model

Scientists and engineers are investigating the use of artificial reefs to repopulate damaged coral reefs. Engineers design physical models, such as concrete blocks and 3-D printed coral skeletons, that will attract algae and free-floating baby coral polyps and begin a new reef.

25. What criteria and constraints do engineers need to consider when designing and constructing a physical reef model?

Divers are setting up concrete reef balls to build an artificial reef.

26. Describe ways that engineers can test different models to determine the one best suited for forming a new reef.

Continue Your Exploration

Name: _____   Date: _____

Check out the path below or go online to choose one of the other paths shown.

| Systems and Organ Donation | • Biosphere 2
 • Hands-On Labs ✋
 • Propose Your Own Path | Go online to choose one of these other paths. |

The human body is a complex system. Interactions among all your body systems are necessary for your body to breathe, play soccer, digest your lunch, and study for a test. But sometimes a component, such as a heart, lung, or kidney, is damaged because of injury or disease, disrupting body system interactions and functions.

Transplantation

A failing tissue or organ can be replaced with one that is healthy. This procedure is called *transplantation*. A tissue or organ from a donor is transplanted to the body of the recipient. Donor tissues and organs, such as skin, bone, or a heart, can come from people who have agreed to donate them after they die. It is also possible to remove some tissues and organs, such as bone marrow and kidneys, from living donors.

A donor is evaluated as a match for the transplant recipient by blood or tissue analysis. The diseased organ, such as a heart, is surgically removed from the recipient and replaced with the healthy organ from the donor.

Heart Transplant Procedure

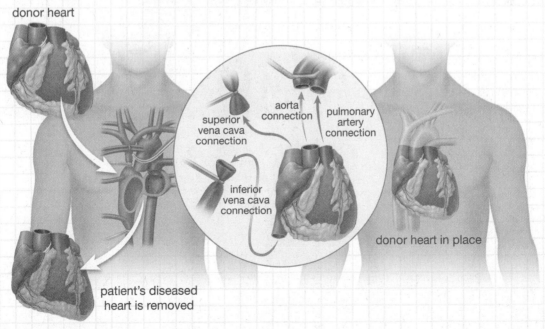

donor heart

superior vena cava connection

aorta connection

pulmonary artery connection

inferior vena cava connection

donor heart in place

patient's diseased heart is removed

Credit: Mayo Foundation for Medical Education and Research

Continue Your Exploration

1. Explain how the failure of one organ can affect the healthy function of the entire body system.

2. The immune system is a subsystem of the body that fights against infection. It recognizes the cells that make up a person's body but attacks invaders, such as bacteria and viruses. How might the function of this system affect tissue and organ transplant success?

Soliciting and Identifying Donors

Unfortunately, there is a shortage of tissue and organs available for donation. A well-organized donation system can maximize the chances of matching people willing to donate with compatible recipients, and ensure rapid delivery of donated organs to waiting recipients. Educating the public about the importance of tissue and organ donation can help to increase the pool of potential donors.

These organ donor family members are making "floragraphs" that will become part of the Donate Life Rose Parade float. The floragraphs honor loved ones who donated tissues or organs to save a life.

3. **Discuss** With a partner, brainstorm ways to improve matches between donors and recipients, and inform the public about the need for tissue and organ donors.

4. **Collaborate** Work in groups to research and learn about organ or tissue donation related to a specific disease. Create a multimedia presentation that describes the disease, the body systems affected, and the transplantation procedure.

© Houghton Mifflin Harcourt Publishing Company • Image Credits: ©Brian Cahn/ZUMA Press, Inc./Alamy

Can You Explain It?

Name: _____ **Date:** _____

How can this model help scientists study natural systems?

EVIDENCE NOTEBOOK

Refer to the notes in your Evidence Notebook to help you construct an explanation for how Biosphere 2 can help scientists study natural systems.

1. State your claim. Make sure your claim fully explains how Biosphere 2 can help scientists study natural systems.

2. Summarize the evidence you have gathered to support your claim and explain your reasoning.

Checkpoints

Answer the following questions to check your understanding of the lesson.

Use the diagram to answer questions 3 and 4.

3. Kidneys are components of the urinary system, a subsystem that filters waste from the blood. A kidney is made up of millions of smaller units, called *nephrons*. Based on this information, which of the statements could be true? Select all that apply.

   A. A nephron is a subsystem.

   B. A kidney is a subsystem.

   C. A kidney is an organ system

   D. A kidney is an organ.

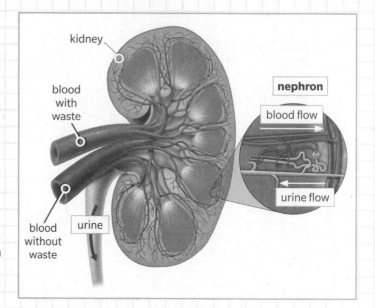

4. The human body has two kidneys, one on each side of the body. Failure of one kidney will / will not result in failure of the urinary system. Failure of both kidneys will / will not require a(n) tissue / organ transplant.

Use the photo to answer Questions 5-6.

5. Palm Jumeirah is a human-engineered island made of sea-floor sand constructed into the shape of a palm tree. Millions of tons of rock were placed around the island to protect it from waves and storms. Draw lines to connect a change caused by the Palm Jumeirah construction to the Earth subsystem affected.

The rocky barriers have changed wave patterns.		geosphere
The shape has led to increased algae and mosquitoes.		anthroposphere
The islands provide shopping, hotels, houses, and restaurants.		hydrosphere
The islands have caused increased erosion of beaches on the coast.		biosphere

6. The Palm Jumeirah is an example of the anthroposphere / geosphere. This structure is likely to have a positive /negative effect on the health of the Earth system.

Interactive Review

Complete this section to review the main concepts of the lesson.

A system is a set of interacting parts that work together. A natural system is a system that occurs in nature.

A. Describe the features that define a system.

Organisms are living systems made up of subsystems that interact to perform functions.

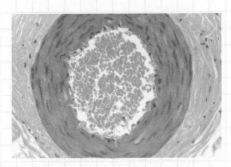

B. Construct a diagram or concept map to describe the subsystems that make up a multicellular organism.

Earth is a system made up of subsystems that interact to make life on Earth possible.

C. Explain why a change to one of Earth's subsystems can have an effect on other Earth subsystems.

Models can be used to study and predict changes to natural systems.

D. Why might scientists use a model of a natural system to predict results of interactions instead of studying the system directly?

Cells Are Living Systems

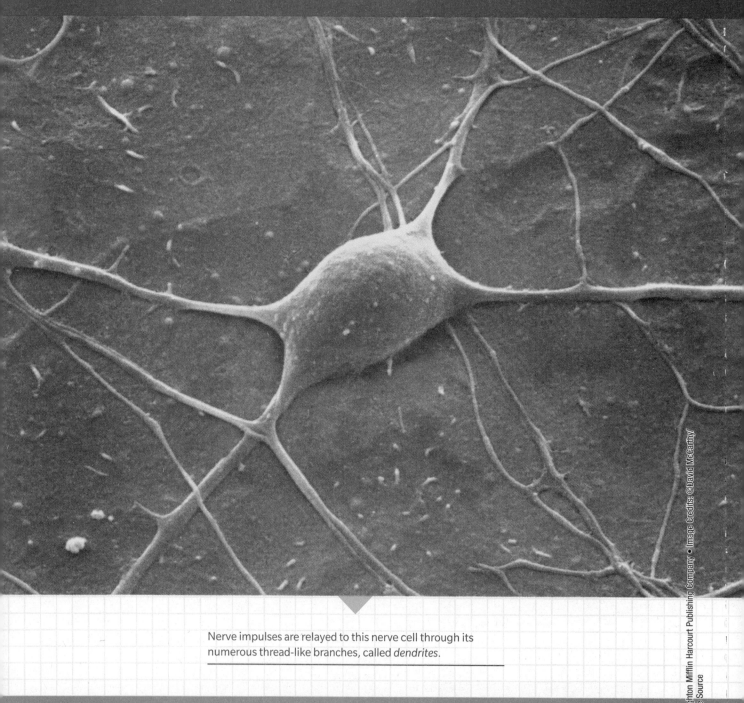

Nerve impulses are relayed to this nerve cell through its numerous thread-like branches, called *dendrites*.

Explore First

Modeling System Interactions Cut a ten-word sentence into its different words and mix the pieces. Put the sentence back in order. Next, remove two words. Does the sentence make sense? Return the removed pieces and arrange the words in a different order. Does the sentence make sense? Discuss why or why not.

CAN YOU EXPLAIN IT?

How does a virus make you sick?

The virus particles (red) attacking this bacterium need a host cell in order to reproduce, or *replicate*.

Do you remember the last time you had a cold? Your runny nose and scratchy throat were signs that your body was responding to an infection caused by a virus. Different types of viruses can infect bacterial, plant, and animal cells.

1. Look at the photo of the viruses attacking the bacterium. What can you conclude about the relative sizes of the virus particles and the host cell?

2. **Discuss** Brainstorm ways that a virus can penetrate the human body's protective boundaries.

EVIDENCE NOTEBOOK As you explore the lesson, gather evidence to explain how a virus makes you sick.

Identifying Cells

When you were very young, you may have played with blocks. You could build almost anything from these blocks —from an insect to a tree or even a person. But, did you know that nature has its own building blocks? Unlike the blocks you played with as a child, the "blocks," or *cells*, that make up all living things can grow, move, and change.

Living Things Are Made of Cells

What makes living things different from nonliving things? The *cell theory* is one way to define living things. The theory states that all living things are made of one or more cells. These cells divide to produce new, identical cells. In this way, all cells are produced only from existing cells. Nonliving things are not made of cells.

Other characteristics are used to define living things. Living things grow, use energy, respond to the environment, and reproduce to make more of their own kind. They can be unicellular, such as bacteria, paramecia, and organisms called *archaeans* that live in extreme environments. Multicellular plants, fungi, and animals are also living things. Nonliving things, such as rocks, oxygen, and water, do not grow, reproduce, or behave in response to the environment.

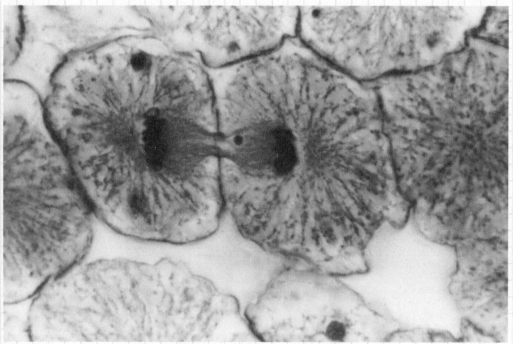

This light microscope image shows two new cells resulting from the division of the original cell.

3. Discuss Why is the cell theory an important tool for classifying unknown objects?

Microscopes Are Used to Observe Cells

Most cells are too small to see with the unaided eye. Because of their extremely small size, most cells can be observed only by using technology, such as a microscope. A microscope allows visualization of cells and cell structures that is not possible with the human eye.

Scientists use several types of microscopes to view cells. For example, light microscopes form magnified images by directing light through thin layers of cells and one or more lenses. Light microscopes can be used to view living or dead specimens. Electron microscopes form images with a beam of electrons. Electron microscopes can only be used to view dead specimens, but provide much greater magnification and visualization of details within the cell than light microscopes.

A butterfly's wing is made up of thousands of scales. Here, wing scales are visualized at 10 times larger than actual size and 100 times larger than actual size using an electron microscope.

4. The magnified photos show *more / less* detail of *smaller / larger* portions of the butterfly wing.

5. The invention of the microscope resulted in the discovery of cells and the development of the cell theory. How does this demonstrate the relationship between science and technology?

Observe Magnified Objects

These images show three different objects as they appear when observed through a microscope. As you explore the images, think about how cells relate to each object.

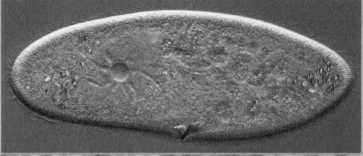

Paramecium A paramecium is an organism made up of a single cell. Tiny hairlike structures, called *cilia*, surround the cell. The cilia beat back and forth, allowing the paramecium to sweep prey microorganisms into its cell mouth.

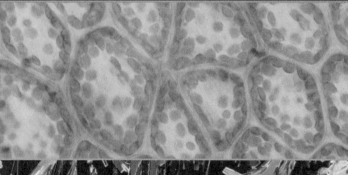

Plant Plants use sunlight to make their own food. The leaf of a plant is an organ made up of specialized cells that contain the structures that absorb sunlight.

Glucose Glucose is a simple sugar made of carbon, hydrogen, and oxygen atoms. Each of these crystals is a grain of sugar.

6. Decide whether each object is a living or a nonliving thing.

   A. Paramecium _____

   B. Plant _____

   C. Glucose _____

7. Select one of the objects in the table. Use evidence to write an argument for why you think the object is a living or a nonliving thing.

EVIDENCE NOTEBOOK

8. Viruses are not made of cells, but they do respond to their environments. They have their own genetic material, but need a host cell to reproduce. Do you think a virus is a living or a nonliving thing? Record your evidence.

Hands-On Lab

Observe Cells with a Microscope

Use a microscope to observe objects and determine if they are made of cells. Microscopes use lenses to magnify objects. The way that the lenses bend light toward your eyes makes the objects appear larger. The scale on a microscope at which you are viewing an object is called *magnification*.

Procedure and Analysis

STEP 1 Describe an investigation that you could conduct with the materials provided that would demonstrate that living things are made of cells and nonliving things are not made of cells. What data would be collected and what evidence might the data provide about living things and cells?

> ### MATERIALS
> - celery stalk
> - celery leaf
> - cork, thin slice
> - eyedropper
> - human hair
> - light microscope
> - microscope slides with coverslips
> - pond water
> - sand
> - tissue paper
> - water
>
>

STEP 2 On a separate sheet of paper, build a data table to collect data from your investigation. Include fields to record data from observations without a microscope, with 10x magnification, and with 40x magnification.

STEP 3 Look at the cork sample without a microscope and record your observations.

STEP 4 Put the cork sample on a slide and add a drop of water. Carefully place the coverslip on the slide so that the cork sample is in the middle.

STEP 5 Make sure that the 10x lens of the microscope is in place. Put the prepared slide on the microscope stage.

STEP 6 Look through the microscope's eyepieces. Adjust the position of the lens until the image of the cork is sharp.

STEP 7 Observe the cork. Write your observations in the 10x column of the table.

STEP 8 Now click the 40x lens into place. Use only the fine focus (never the coarse focus) to adjust the image. View the cork sample and write your observations in the 40x column of the table.

STEP 9 Repeat Steps 3–8 with the remaining samples.

STEP 10 Evaluate the data you collected. Which items contained cells? Which objects do you think were part of living things? Which objects do you think were part of nonliving things?

STEP 11 How do your observations support the cell theory?

STEP 12 **Engineer It** Identify the needs filled by the microscope in this activity. What are the limitations of the microscope you are using?

Draw to Scale

To draw microscopic and very small objects it is useful to *scale up*, or calculate the size of the objects to be larger than what they actually are. The table below shows the actual sizes and scaled up sizes of a few cell types.

object	actual size (mm)	size in mm if scaled up 100x	size in cm if scaled up 100x
bacterium	0.002	0.2	0.02
cheek cell	0.050	5	0.5
onion cell	0.250	25	2.5

Credit: Adapted from Amazing Cells by Maureen Munn et al. Copyright © 2007 by University of Washington. Adapted and reproduced by permission of Maureen Munn, Ph.D. and Phyllis Harvey-Bushel Ed. D.

9. Use a metric ruler to draw each of the cells scaled up 100 times in either millimeters or centimeters. Compare and contrast the sizes of the cells with each other, an onion, and a person.

Analyzing Cell Systems

Types of Cells and Their Structures

Every cell is a system made up of interacting parts. There are different types of cells, but they all have some structures in common. The **cell membrane** surrounds and protects the cell. The cell membrane regulates the matter that enters and exits the cell. Cytoplasm is all the content inside of the cell membrane except for the nucleus. Genetic material contains all the information a cell needs to function.

Some cell types also contain **organelles,** membrane-bound structures in the cytoplasm that each perform a specific function. Mitochondria, chloroplasts, and nuclei are examples of organelles. Not every cell contains every type of organelle, and different types of cells may have different organelles and other specialized structures. Although many kinds of cells exist, all cells can be organized into two categories: prokaryotes and eukaryotes.

Prokaryotic Cells

A prokaryotic cell contains its genetic material in the cytoplasm. Most prokaryotic cells do not have membrane-bound organelles, although they do have other structures called *ribosomes* that make proteins. Prokaryotic cells are unicellular organisms. Bacteria and archaeans are prokaryotes.

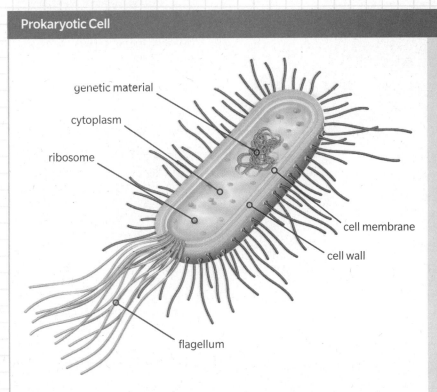

Prokaryotic Cell

genetic material
cytoplasm
ribosome
cell membrane
cell wall
flagellum

genetic material Genetic material contains information that directs all of the cell's functions.

cytoplasm The cytoplasm is all the content inside the cell membrane except for the nucleus.

ribosome Ribosomes make proteins inside the cytoplasm.

cell membrane The cell membrane surrounds and protects the cell and controls what materials go into and out of it.

cell wall The cell wall provides structural support for some prokaryotic cells.

flagella These projections move the prokaryote through its environment.

10. Which structure is the boundary of this cell system?

Eukaryotic Cells

Eukaryotic cells are generally larger and more complex than prokaryotic cells. In a eukaryotic cell, genetic material is enclosed in a membrane-bound organelle called the **nucleus.** Eukaryotic cells also have additional membrane-bound organelles.

Animals and plants are both made of eukaryotic cells. Both have organelles called **mitochondria,** which convert the energy stored in food to a form of energy that cells can use. Plant cells and animal cells also have some different structures. For example, plants make their own food using a process called *photosynthesis*. Therefore, plant cells have organelles called **chloroplasts,** where photosynthesis occurs. Animals do not make their own food, so animal cells do not have chloroplasts. Each plant cell also has a rigid **cell wall** that supports the cell. The extra support of a cell wall is not needed in animal cells because most animals have some type of skeleton that supports the body.

Animal Cell

An animal cell has some of the same structures as a prokaryotic cell, such as a cell membrane and cytoplasm, and some different structures.

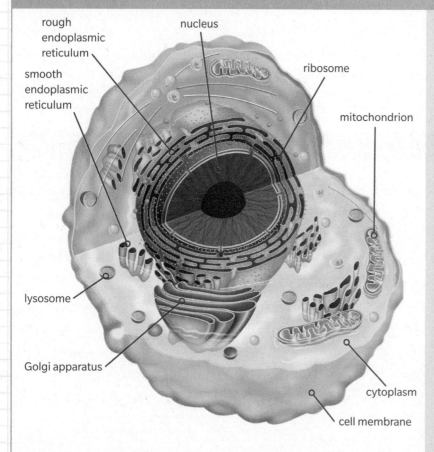

rough endoplasmic reticulum

nucleus

ribosome

smooth endoplasmic reticulum

mitochondrion

lysosome

Golgi apparatus

cytoplasm

cell membrane

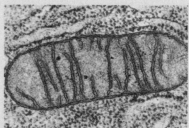

Nucleus The cell nucleus contains genetic information that gives instructions for making proteins and other materials the cell needs.

Mitochondrion This organelle converts energy stored in food into a form the cell can use. Cells that need a lot of energy, such as muscle cells, have more mitochondria than do cells that need less energy, such as bone cells.

Rough ER The rough ER is located near the nucleus and contains ribosomes on its surface. It is involved in making and processing proteins.

Smooth ER The smooth ER does not contain ribosomes. It makes fat-based molecules called lipids that are used to make membranes.

Golgi apparatus The Golgi apparatus takes proteins from the ER and moves them to different parts of the cell.

Lysosome These structures contain powerful chemicals known as enzymes that break down food and recycle proteins, carbohydrates, lipids, and nucleic acids inside the cell.

Plant Cell

In addition to a cell membrane, cytoplasm, nucleus, and mitochondria, a plant cell also has a cell wall and chloroplasts.

Chloroplast In the cells of plants and a few other kinds of organisms, chloroplasts capture energy from sunlight and change it into food that stores energy for the cell to use.

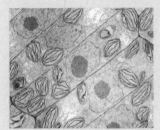

Cell wall A cell wall surrounds the entire plant cell, including its cell membrane, and supports the plant cell. Most bacterial cells, which are prokaryotic, also have cell walls.

Vacuole A large central vacuole is bound by a membrane and contains materials and waste. It also maintains adequate pressure inside the plant cell.

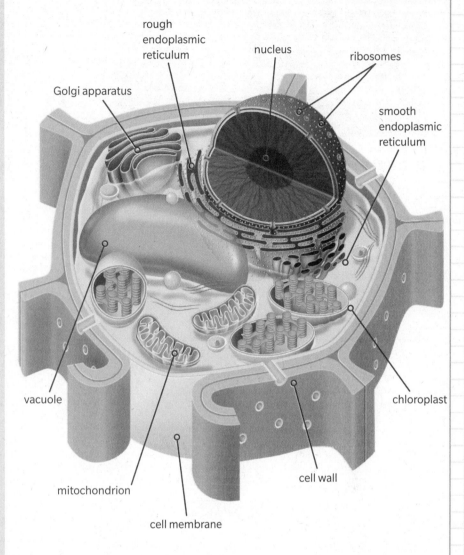

rough endoplasmic reticulum

nucleus

ribosomes

Golgi apparatus

smooth endoplasmic reticulum

vacuole

chloroplast

mitochondrion

cell wall

cell membrane

11. Read these cell observations. In the space next to each answer choice, write whether the cells described are prokaryotic cells, animal cells, plant cells, or there is not enough information to determine.

   A. Cell has a membrane and ribosomes but no organelles. _____

   B. Cell has many chloroplasts. _____

   C. Cell has a cell membrane and mitochondria but no cell wall. _____

   D. Cell has a nucleus. _____

   E. Cell has a nucleus and cell wall. _____

Identify Different Cell Systems

12. Define each cell system. Identify the cell system boundary, two or more components, and one or more functions that result from system interactions.

bacteria cells	fish embryo cell	moss leaf cells
Boundary:	Boundary:	Boundary:
Components:	Components:	Components:
Functions:	Functions:	Functions:

13. What types of inputs and outputs do these cell systems share?

_____

_____

_____

_____

_____

_____

EVIDENCE NOTEBOOK

14. Viruses inject their own DNA into a host cell. The viral DNA uses the host cell's components to make more viruses. How might this affect the function of the host cell system? Record your evidence.

Modeling Cells

Imagine that a friend asks you how the sizes of planets in our solar system compare to each other. A map of the solar system would show you the planets and the shapes of their orbits, but it would be difficult to see how their sizes compare. However, if you built a model of the solar system, you could show your friend many things about the solar system. You could show planet sizes in relation to each other and to the sun, and you could show how far away the planets are from each other.

Scientists use both two-dimensional (2D) and three-dimensional (3D) models to study cells. Examples of a 2D cell model are an illustration or a photograph. Examples of a 3D cell model are a physical model that can be touched and moved around, or a computer model that includes the dimensions of width, height, and depth.

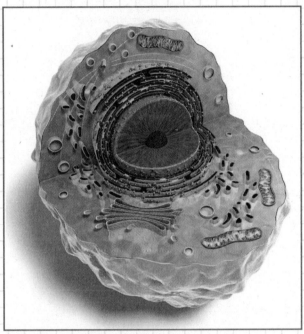

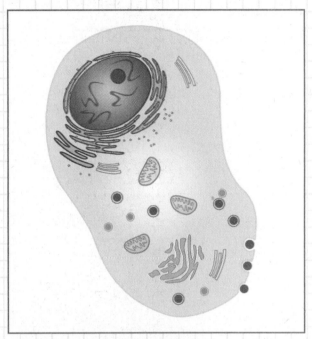

This illustration uses perspective to represent three dimensions of a cell.

This illustration is flat and represents two dimensions of a cell.

15. There are advantages and disadvantages to different models. Examine the two models, note the types of information each provides, and list the pros and cons of using each model.

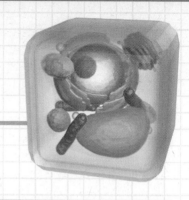

Hands-On Lab

Use Cell Models to Investigate Cell Size

Use large and small cubes of gelatin to model cell function in cells of different sizes. Use evidence to support an explanation of how cell size affects function.

The gelatin cubes that you will work with represent a model of a cell. Using a cube allows you to easily calculate its dimensions, such as its surface area and volume. A cell's surface area-to-volume ratio is an important factor in its functioning.

MATERIALS

- beaker, 250 mL (2)
- calculator (if desired)
- container, plastic, 473 mL (2)
- gelatin cubes, prepared (1 large and 27 small)
- ruler, metric
- stopwatch or clock with second hand
- water, warm

Procedure and Analysis

STEP 1 Work with a partner. Measure the length of each side of the large gelatin cube and one of the smaller cubes. (All of the smaller cubes are the same size). Record the measurements in the data table.

	Cube sides (cm)	Surface area (cm²)	Volume (cm³)	SA:V ratio	Time to dissolve
Large cube					
Smaller cube					

STEP 2 Place the large cube in one of the plastic containers. Place the 27 smaller cubes in the other container.

STEP 3 Ask your teacher to fill your beakers with warm water to the same level. Then pour the water from the beakers into both plastic containers at the same time. Make sure all the gelatin cubes are submerged in the water. Start the timer. If any water has spilled, clean it up immediately to avoid slips.

STEP 4
Do the Math While you wait for the cubes to dissolve, calculate the surface area, volume, and surface area-to-volume ratio for the large cube and the smaller cubes. Enter this data into the data table.

To calculate the surface area (SA) of a cube, first multiply the cube's length (L) by its width (W). Then multiply the answer by 6 (for the 6 sides of the cube).

Formula: SA = L × W × 6

To calculate the volume (V) of the cube, multiply the length (L) by the width (W) by the height (H).

Formula: V = L × W × H

A ratio compares two quantities. One way to write the surface area-to-volume ratio is to use a colon between the surface area (SA) and the volume (V).

SA to V ratio = SA : V

STEP 5 Record the length of time it took for the gelatin cubes to completely dissolve.

STEP 6 Which of the cubes has the largest total surface area and the largest total volume? Which has the highest surface area-to-volume ratio?

STEP 7 Describe the relationship between surface area-to-volume ratio and the time it took for the cubes to dissolve.

STEP 8 Remember that all cells must take in materials and get rid of wastes through the cell membrane. Think about how the surface area-to-volume ratio affected the time it took for the different-sized cubes to dissolve. What can you infer about the relationship between the surface area-to-volume ratio and the movement of materials into and out of a cell?

Language SmArts
Explain Limits to Cell Size

Imagine you are looking at a small mouse. You know that both the mouse and your own body are made of cells because all living things are made of cells.

Cell sizes can vary based on their function. For example, red blood cells that transport blood throughout your body are small. But muscle cells in your leg are much larger. A human contains more than 37 trillion cells. Given how much larger you are compared to a mouse, how do your cells compare in size?

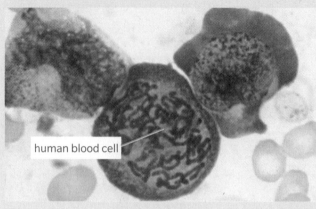

human blood cell

This purple human red blood cell is roughly 6-8 μm. One micron, or 1 μm, is 1/1,000 the size of 1mm.

16. Humans must have *more / larger* 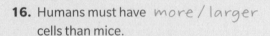 cells than mice.

17. Given your answer, explain your reasoning for the difference in cell size or cell number between humans and mice.

_____

_____

_____

_____

_____

_____

18. What problems might result if a cell gets too large? Use evidence from your cell modeling lab to explain why cells are unable to perform important functions if they become too large.

_____

_____

_____

_____

_____

_____

_____

_____

EVIDENCE NOTEBOOK

19. Viruses are much smaller than living cells. Many viruses form inside a single cell, causing the cell to burst open and die. How might this affect the function of the organism as a system? Record your evidence.

Continue Your Exploration

Name: _____   Date: _____

Check out the path below or go online to choose one of the other paths shown.

| People in Science | • **Making a Microscope** • **Hands-On Labs** • **Propose Your Own Path** | *Go online to choose one of these other paths.* |

Lynn Margulis, Biologist

Lynn Margulis (1938–2011) was a biologist who made many important contributions to science. Her most well-known contribution was her proposal in 1966 that eukaryotic cells evolved through the process of endosymbiosis. She proposed that billions of years ago, smaller prokaryotes began living inside larger host prokaryotic cells. In some cases, smaller prokaryotes entered larger cells as parasites. In others, smaller cells were engulfed by larger cells. Margulis proposed that mitochondria and chloroplasts of today's eukaryotic cells are descended from free-living bacteria.

Eventually Margulis outlined her ideas in her 1970 book *Origin of Eukaryotic Cells*. Most scientists of the time were skeptical of the ideas because they thought the organelles of eukaryotic cells evolved from materials found inside the cells.

Today, most scientists accept Margulis's hypothesis. She and other scientists showed that, like a cell nucleus, mitochondria and chloroplasts contain DNA. Also, the DNA of mitochondria and chloroplasts is different from the DNA in a cell's nucleus. Instead, the DNA of mitochondria and chloroplasts resembles the DNA of bacteria.

American biologist Lynn Margulis at work in a greenhouse in the 1990s.

Continue Your Exploration

1. Which statements provide evidence to support Lynn Margulis's hypothesis of endosymbiosis? Arrange the statements below into the order that accurately shows the sequence of events described in Margulis's hypothesis by writing the number 1, 2, 3, or 4 next to each statement.

_____ Prokaryotes inside other prokaryotes evolved into organelles.

_____ Prokaryotes lived inside other prokaryotes in a symbiotic relationship.

_____ Prokaryotes that had engulfed other prokaryotes evolved into eukaryotes.

_____ Free-living prokaryotes engulfed other free-living prokaryotes.

2. How do the findings of Margulis and other scientists—that mitochondria and chloroplasts have their own DNA, like a cell's nucleus—support the hypothesis of endosymbiosis?

3. Explain how Lynn Margulis's hypothesis changed scientific ideas about cell development.

4. **Collaborate** Research the prokaryotic organism that most likely evolved into a chloroplast. Develop a model of a chloroplast and the prokaryote and describe the similarities and differences in the structure and function of individual components and the whole system.

Can You Explain It?

Name: _____   **Date:** _____

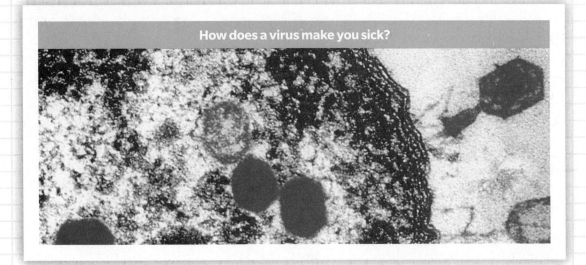

How does a virus make you sick?

EVIDENCE NOTEBOOK

Refer to the notes in your Evidence Notebook to help explain how a virus makes you sick.

1. State your claim. Make sure your claim fully explains how a virus makes you sick.

2. Summarize the evidence you have gathered to support your claim and explain your reasoning.

Checkpoints

Answer the following questions to check your understanding of the lesson.

Use the photograph to answer Question 3.

3. Study the photograph. What would happen to these cells if the green components were not functional? Select all that apply.

   A. The cells would not have a source of energy.

   B. The cells would function normally.

   C. The cells would eventually die.

   D. The cells would not be able to control inputs and outputs.

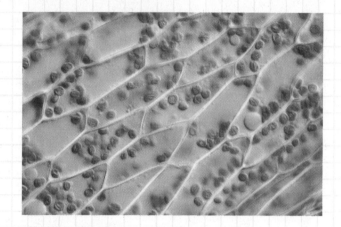

---

4. If a cell's surface area-to-volume ratio increased from 3:1 to 4:1, what impact would that have on the transport of materials across the cell membrane?

   A. it would be unchanged

   B. transport would increase

   C. transport would decrease

   D. none of the above

Use the illustration to answer Questions 5 and 6.

5. An analogy is a model of a relationship. Match each cell organelle to the analogy of its function.

nucleus	power plant
cell membrane	control center
mitochondrion	solar panel
chloroplast	border between countries

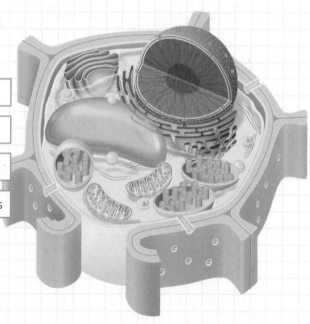

6. The cell system shown in the diagram is a
   prokaryotic / eukaryotic cell. The
   evidence supporting this is that the cell has
   chloroplasts / flagella and a
   nucleus / cell wall.

Interactive Review

Complete this section to review the main concepts of the lesson.

All living things are made of cells.

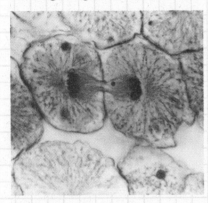

A. List two statements of the cell theory.

All cells are systems made of components that interact to perform functions.

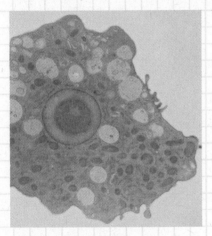

B. Draw a concept map to show the parts that make up an animal cell system.

Examining 3D models of cells can enhance understanding of how cell structures work together to maximize function.

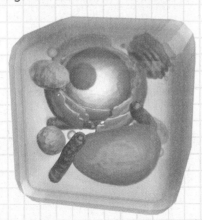

C. Explain how using 3D models of cells can help scientists gain a better understanding of cell structure and function.

Plants Are Living Systems

Dragon's blood trees have a wide, dense canopy of leaves that protects the soil below from the hot sun.

Explore First

Modeling Leaves Cut two identical, leaf-shaped pieces from a paper towel. Use a spray bottle to wet, but not soak, both shapes equally with water. Wrap one in wax paper and set both near a sunny window or other warm location. Which "leaf" do you think will dry faster? Record your observations at the end of class.

Go online to view the digital version of the Hands-On Lab for this lesson and to download additional lab resources.

CAN YOU EXPLAIN IT?

How can the onyanga survive in the harsh conditions of the Namib Desert?

The onyanga grows in the Namib desert, where there is little rain but regular, dense fog develops at night.

For many hundreds of years—and possibly even thousands of years—this plant has been growing where not much else can grow. It grows only two leaves that become ragged and torn over time, a stem, and roots. It may not look like much, but it can go without rain for up to 5 years. The largest onyanga plants are estimated to be nearly 2,500 years old!

1. **Discuss** Study the photo of the onyanga. Record as many observations as you can about the plant.

EVIDENCE NOTEBOOK As you explore the lesson, gather evidence to help you explain how the body systems of the onyanga help it survive in the desert.

Exploring Plant Body Systems

Plants live on every continent on Earth. They live in lush forests and expansive grasslands. They also live in places you might not expect, such as dry deserts and frozen tundra. They range in size from the tallest giant sequoia trees, reaching more than 80 meters, to the smallest flowering plant, which can fit on the tip of your finger.

All plants are multicellular. They are also eukaryotes—their cells contain membrane-bound organelles, including a nucleus that contains the cell's genetic information. All plants have cells with cell walls and large vacuoles. All plants use energy from sunlight to make their own food by a process called *photosynthesis*.

This maple tree has a central stem, called a *trunk*, that connects the roots to the branches of the tree.

The root system of the saguaro cactus is shallow, but it reaches out as far as the plant is tall.

The water lily's broad, flat leaves float on the water to maximize the amount of sunlight they can capture.

2. **Discuss** With a partner, gather information from the text and the photos to compare the plants shown above. Record your observations in the table.

Similarities	Differences

The Plant Body System

Plants can be divided into two major groups based on the structure and function of their body systems. Most of the land plants on Earth today have a vascular system. A *vascular system* transports materials and provides support to the plant body. Plants that have a vascular system are called *vascular plants*. Plants that do not have a vascular system are called *nonvascular plants*.

Plant Cells

Like all living things, plants are made of cells. Plant cells have rigid cell walls, which help to provide structure and support for the plant.

Plant Tissues

The cells in a vascular plant are organized into three tissue types. *Dermal tissue* protects the plant, *vascular tissue* transports materials, and *ground tissue* provides support and storage.

Plant Organs

Leaves, stems, roots, and flowers are all plant organs made up of the three tissue types. For example, the stem is protected by dermal tissue. Inside the stem, the vascular tissue that transports water and nutrients is surrounded by ground tissue. Ground tissue gives the stem support and stores materials.

cell structure

Cell

leaf

shoot system

stem

organ

tissue

Plant Organ Systems

Plant organs are organized into two organ systems. The *shoot system* includes the leaves, stems, and flowers. The *root system* takes up water and nutrients from the soil. These two systems work together to deliver water and nutrients to all parts of the plant body.

root system

roots

3. Use the diagram of the vascular plant as evidence to support the claim that the root system and shoot system interact to deliver water and nutrients to all parts of the plant body.

4. The onyanga has a wide, shallow root system. How might this type of root system help the onyanga collect nightly fog? Record your evidence.

Analyze a Plant Body System

Sundews live in habitats where sunlight and water are plentiful, but the soil has few nutrients. Like most plants, sundews make their own food using energy from sunlight. Unlike most plants, sundews also capture and digest insects. Sundew leaves are covered with tentacle-like structures that contain a sweet, sticky substance. Insects attracted to the sundew for a tasty meal get trapped in the leaf and are digested by the plant.

When an insect lands on a sundew, it gets stuck on the sticky leaf. The leaf curls around the trapped insect, which is digested by the plant.

Explore Online

5. Why do you think sundews need to capture insects?

A. The sundew is unable to make enough food.

B. The insects provide water to the plant.

C. The sundew is protecting itself from insects.

D. The insects provide nutrients that are missing from the soil.

6. Sundews have weakly developed roots. Why do you think sundews do not need strong roots?

_____

_____

_____

_____

7. How does the structure of the sundew leaf relate to its function?

_____

_____

_____

_____

_____

Describing How Plant Systems Process Nutrients

Plants bodies are systems that perform all the processes needed for a plant to live. Plants need sunlight, water, and carbon dioxide to make and transport the food they use as a source of matter. They also need oxygen to convert the food to energy that is used by all parts of the plant. Nutrients from the soil, such as nitrogen and phosphorus, are used for cellular processes and growth. All of these processes produce unwanted products, so plants also need to get rid of wastes to stay healthy.

Making Food

Like you, plants need food that cells can use for energy. But unlike you, plants do not get their food by eating. Instead, plants make their own food by the process of photosynthesis. *Photosynthesis* is the process that uses energy from sunlight to convert water molecules and carbon dioxide into sugars and oxygen. A **leaf** is the plant organ that is the main site of photosynthesis. The sugars produced in leaf cells are transported from the leaves to all parts of the plant's body.

Inputs and Outputs of Photosynthesis

8. Complete the diagram by labeling the inputs and outputs of the process of photosynthesis. Use evidence from the text.

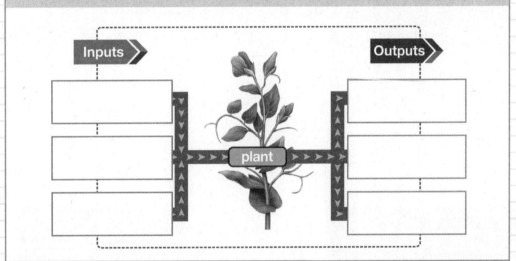

 9. Engineer It Solar cells are devices that collect energy from sunlight and convert it into electricity. What plant structure might engineers look at when they are designing the way that solar cells are arranged? Explain your reasoning.

Moving Materials

Materials move through a plant through two kinds of vascular tissue—xylem and phloem. Water and dissolved nutrients enter the plant through the **roots**, organs that absorb water and dissolved nutrients from soil. Roots also anchor the plant in the ground. Roots connect to **stems**, organs that transport nutrients to all parts of the plant body and provide support to the plant. Water moves from the roots to the stems through tube-shaped cells in the xylem tissue. Sugars made during photosynthesis move throughout the plant in the phloem.

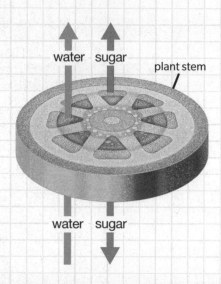

water   sugar

plant stem

water   sugar

Compare Root Systems

10. Using the word bank, complete the Venn diagram by entering the functions you think best describe the root systems.

WORD BANK

- absorbs nutrients
- stores nutrients
- drought tolerant
- absorbs water
- anchors plant
- protects soil

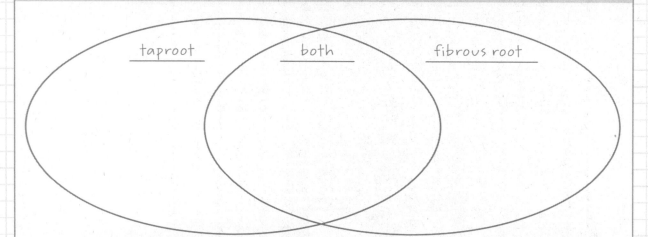

taproot   both   fibrous root

taproot

Some plants have a root system called a taproot. As you can see in the photo, these plants have one large main root structure with many smaller branch roots. Taproots can grow deep into the soil.

fibrous root

Other plants have a fibrous root system, in which many branching roots grow close to the soil surface. Fibrous roots can spread wide and form mats that anchor the plant very firmly in the soil.

Hands-On Lab
Observe Transport

You will compare and contrast the movement of water through the stems of two different plants.

MATERIALS
- asparagus spears
- broccoli stems
- clear plastic cups, 16 oz (2)
- graduated cylinder
- knife
- red food coloring
- stir stick

Procedure

STEP 1 Fill two 16 oz cups with 100 mL of water each. Add 10–15 drops of red food coloring and mix thoroughly.

STEP 2 Use the knife to cut 8 cm sections of the broccoli stem and the asparagus spears. Be sure to cut the stems horizontally.

STEP 3 Place one or two pieces of broccoli stem in one cup and one or two pieces of asparagus spears in the other cup. Be sure the stems stand upright in the water and will not fall over.

STEP 4 Allow the stems to sit in the water for 24 hours. Cut your stems at 1–2 cm intervals to see how far the water traveled up the stems.

STEP 5 Record your observations in the data table below.

Asparagus	Broccoli

Analysis

STEP 6 How do your observations from this activity provide evidence for the function of a plant's vascular system?

STEP 7 Through which vascular tissue did the water move in the broccoli and asparagus stems?

Disposing of Wastes

Plants produce waste as a result of cell processes, such as photosynthesis. Water, carbon dioxide, and oxygen enter and exit a plant through tiny openings in the leaf surface, called stomata (*sing.* stoma).

Plants also need to get rid of unwanted substances, such as pollutants, that may enter their systems through water. Some plants store wastes in living cells, such as leaves. These unwanted materials are removed when the leaves fall from the plant.

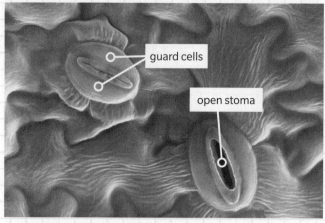

The size, shape, and placement of stomata allow water and gases to efficiently move in and out of the plant.

11. A plant system must balance its need for water with its need for carbon dioxide and oxygen. If too much water is lost, the stomata will close. How does this affect a plant's ability to regulate levels of carbon dioxide and oxygen?

12. Discuss What would likely occur if most of a plant's stomata became blocked? Explain your reasoning.

Language SmArts
Use Observations to Develop an Argument

13. This plant has shallow roots, short stems, and leaves that are covered in fuzzy hairs. In what type of environmental conditions might this plant live? Use your observations as evidence to support your argument.

_____

_____

_____

_____

_____

_____

Describing How Plant Systems Respond to the Environment

Unlike many animals, plants cannot move to a new place when their environment changes. Plant bodies respond to a variety of environmental factors. Many of these responses happen very slowly. Other responses are surprisingly fast! The Venus flytrap will respond to the touch of an insect in a few seconds by snapping its leaf shut. Two factors that plants respond to are light and water.

14. Why do you think it is important for plants to be able to regulate the level of water in their bodies?

Regulating Water

Plants regulate the water in their bodies in response to environmental conditions. Plants do this mostly by opening and closing their stomata. Two guard cells control the opening and closing of each stoma. Stomata open to allow air to move in and out. They close to prevent water loss. Some plant leaves also have a waxy coating that helps prevent water loss. Plants may also store water in their stems, leaves, or roots.

Do the Math

Calculate Stomata Percentage

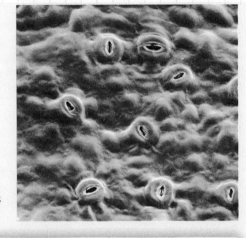

The percentage of stomata on a leaf surface can be calculated using the equation:

$$\text{Stomatal percentage} = \frac{S}{S+E} \times 100$$

where S = the number of stomata and E = the number of epidermis cells, which form the outer layer of a leaf.

Look at the photo of the leaf.

15. Count and write the number of open stomata that you can see. _____

16. If the number of epidermis cells in this area is 120, what is the percentage of stomata in this area of the leaf?

17. Stomata percentage on a plant varies, depending on the environment where the plant lives. What environmental factors might influence the percentage of stomata? Explain your thinking.

137

18. The onyanga opens its stomata only at night for necessary gas exchange. How might this adaptation help the plant survive in its environment? Record your evidence.

Responding to Light and Gravity

Have you ever noticed your houseplant growing toward the window? One way that plants respond to their environment is by growing toward a light source. This process is called *phototropism*. Chemical messengers build up on the shaded side of the plant's stem. These messengers cause the cells to grow longer. As the cells on the shaded side grow longer, they cause the stem to bend toward the light source.

A change in the direction of plant growth in response to gravity is called *gravitropism* or *geotropism*. Most stems grow upward, away from the pull of Earth's gravity. Most roots grow downward, toward the pull of gravity.

19. What advantage do you think growing toward a light source gives a plant?

20. What might happen to a plant if the roots grew away from the pull of Earth's gravity?

Construct an Explanation

21. Water pressure in stems and leaves helps to keep a plant rigid. A plant wilts when there is a lack of water. How do interactions at the cell and tissue levels cause a plant to wilt? Explain your reasoning.

Explore Online

_____

_____

_____

_____

_____

Continue Your Exploration

Name: _____   Date: _____

Check out the path below or go online to choose one of the other paths shown.

| Growing Plants in Space | • **Feeding the World Using Less Water**
 • **Hands-On Labs** 🖐
 • **Propose Your Own Path** | *Go online to choose one of these other paths.* |

The International Space Station is a research laboratory that travels at a speed of 8 kilometers per second and orbits Earth every 90 minutes. Solar panels provide power to the station, and life support systems supply oxygen and remove unwanted gases from the enclosed space. The water supply is supplemented by capturing and recycling the water vapors that enter the cabin when the crew members exhale and sweat! The crew members are researching ways to grow food on the space station in the hope that they will be able to have fresh food available for extended periods of time in space.

An astronaut harvests red romaine lettuce. These plants were grown from seed in the station's plant growth chamber.

© Houghton Mifflin Harcourt Publishing Company • Image Credits: ©Science Source

139

Continue Your Exploration

1. The force of gravity is very weak on the space station, a condition referred to as microgravity. How might microgravity affect the growth of plants on the space station? Select all that apply.

   A. The length and shape of the roots and stems of the plants grown in space might be different than the same plants grown on Earth.

   B. The plant may not be able to absorb and transport water and nutrients in microgravity.

   C. The plant would not be able to respond to light in microgravity.

   D. The growth of the plant would not be affected by microgravity.

2. One of the biggest challenges of long-term space travel is having a sufficient supply of fresh water. Water must be recycled and used sparingly to ensure that the crew will have enough water to drink and to bathe. What types of plants from Earth would be good candidates for food plants for the crew of the space station? Select all that apply.

   A. plants from dense areas of vegetation that are adapted to crowded conditions

   B. plants from dry areas that are adapted to drought conditions

   C. plants from shady areas that are adapted to low light conditions

   D. plants from coastal areas that are adapted to saltwater conditions

3. Do you think the plants on the space station are able to conduct photosynthesis? Explain why or why not.

4. **Collaborate** Research plant growth in space. You may also find out more about the space garden on the International Space Station. Gather information about the types of questions researchers are asking about growing plants in space and the research being conducted to answer these questions. Develop a multimedia presentation or informational brochure that communicates your findings.

Can You Explain It?

Name: _____

Date: _____

How can the onyanga survive in the harsh conditions of the Namib Desert?

EVIDENCE NOTEBOOK

Refer to the notes in your Evidence Notebook to help you construct an explanation of how the onyanga can survive in the Namib Desert.

1. State your claim. Make sure your claim fully explains how the onyanga's body systems help it survive the harsh conditions of the Namib Desert.

2. Summarize the evidence you have gathered to support your claim and explain your reasoning.

Checkpoints

Answer the following questions to check your understanding of the lesson.

Use the photo to answer Questions 3 and 4.

3. Prickly pear cacti live in hot, dry habitats. The spines are modified leaves that do not have stomata. The green stems of the cactus store water and are covered in stomata. The site of photosynthesis in the prickly pear is likely to be the spines / stems.

4. Which statement best describes the relationship between structure and function in the prickly pear cactus? Select all that apply.

   A. The stems are wide to maximize the capture of sunlight.

   B. The spines are narrow because they do not have stomata.

   C. The spines protect the stem from animals that try to eat the cactus.

   D. The stems are wide to maximize the amount of water that can be stored.

Use the photo to answer Questions 5 and 6.

This red mangrove tree has specialized roots, called prop roots, that extend above the ground.

5. The specialized roots of the mangrove tree help the tree to anchor / float in the sandy soil. The aboveground portions deliver gases / sunlight to the roots that are under the water.

6. Mangrove trees live in saline conditions that would kill most other types of plants. How do you think the mangrove tree is able to tolerate this environment?

   A. The mangrove tree needs more salt than other plants to live.

   B. The mangrove tree disposes of salt through its leaves.

   C. Animals that live on the tree eat the salt from the tree.

   D. The mangrove tree does not grow as well as trees that do not live in saltwater conditions.

Interactive Review

Complete this section to review the main concepts of the lesson.

Plants are living systems made up of cells that form tissues, organs, and organ systems.

A. Describe why the interaction of the different components in the plant body are necessary for the plant body system to function.

Plant body systems interact to perform all the functions needed for survival.

B. Draw Make a diagram to explain how a plant's root system and shoot system work together to provide the plant with food, water, and soil nutrients.

Plant body systems respond to the environment.

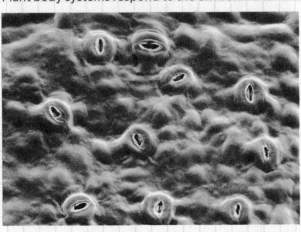

C. Describe the cause-and-effect relationships between conditions in the environment, such as light and a plant's response to light.

Animals Are Living Systems

The pangolin is the only mammal that has scales. The scales protect the pangolin from predators such as leopards and hyenas.

Explore First

Exploring Senses Fill a paper bag with items that have different textures. In groups, take turns feeling one item without looking, and identify what it is. How did each person determine what the item was by only using the sense of touch?

© Houghton Mifflin Harcourt Publishing Company • Image Credits: ©J Dennis Nigel/ Getty Images

Go online to view the digital version of the Hands-On Lab for this lesson and to download additional lab resources.

CAN YOU EXPLAIN IT?

Why is it so difficult to catch a fly?

Houseflies can be found anywhere there are animals. They feed on garbage, manure, or softened food, like this biscuit left on the counter.

1. **Discuss** Have you ever tried to catch a fly? If so, you know that it isn't easy. Look at the photo of the fly. Write down your observations about its body and think about how the parts might be involved in evading your grasp.

 EVIDENCE NOTEBOOK As you explore the lesson, gather evidence to help you explain why it is so difficult to catch a fly.

Analyzing Animal Body Systems

When we think of animals we often think of feathered or furry creatures, but sponges, corals, and worms are animals too. Animals live on land, underground, in freshwater and in salt water—in nearly every place on Earth where there is life. Some animals even live in or on other animals!

The Animal Body

Animal bodies come in many shapes and sizes, but they have some characteristics in common. All animals are multicellular. Animals can have four basic tissue types: nervous, epithelial, connective, and muscle. Nervous tissue functions as a messaging system within the body. Epithelial tissue protects and forms boundaries, and is found in organs such as skin. Connective tissue, including bones and blood, holds parts of the body together and provides support. Muscle tissue produces movement.

The organs in an animal are made up of two or more of these tissue types. For example, the human heart is made up of muscle, nervous, and epithelial tissues. Organs are organized into systems that perform specific functions, such as digestion of food or delivery of oxygen. The types of tissues, organs, and organ systems present in an animal depend on the type of animal and its environment.

2. **Discuss** Look at the photos and read the captions. With a partner, discuss the ways that these animals are similar and the ways they are different.

This **nautilus** moves by "jet propulsion." Water is pulled into its shell and forced out of a muscular, flexible tube.

The unusual looking **okapi** has large, upright ears that can detect the slightest sound.

This **red rock crab** has five pairs of legs that grip rocks and help the crab avoid being swept away by powerful waves.

Digestive and Excretory System Interactions

Animals get the energy they need from food. The *digestive system* and *excretory system* interact to process food and eliminate wastes. Digestion begins with the teeth or other structures that break down food mechanically. Digestive enzymes in the saliva and stomach chemically break down the food, which is absorbed into the bloodstream in the small intestine. Solid wastes are processed and expelled by the large intestine.

The excretory system removes liquid wastes from the body. The skin, lungs, and kidneys are organs in the excretory system. For example, excess salts are released through the skin when an animal sweats. Waste products are filtered from blood as it flows through the kidneys. When you breathe out, or exhale, carbon dioxide and water vapor are released from your lungs.

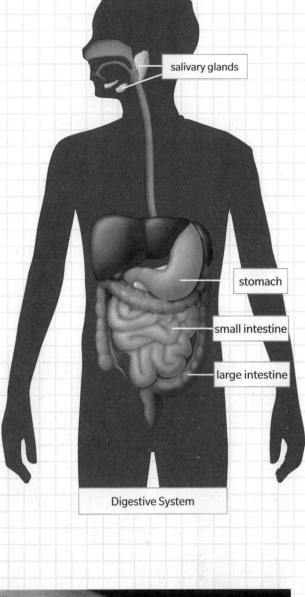

salivary glands

stomach

small intestine

large intestine

Digestive System

3. The crabeater seal is an aquatic mammal that eats krill, tiny shrimp-like crustaceans. It filters the krill from the water as it swims. A tiger shark is a fierce predator that eats a wide variety of prey. Which teeth do you think belong to the *crabeater seal* and which belong to the *tiger shark*? Write the name in the box provided.

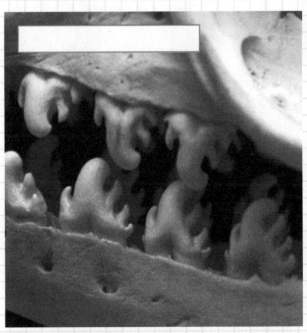

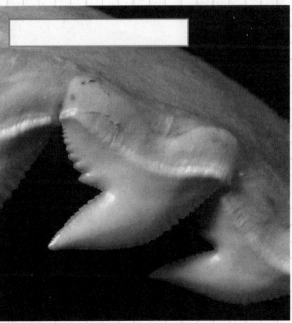

© Houghton Mifflin Harcourt Publishing Company • Image Credits: (l) ©Pat Morris/a•dea.com; (r) ©Matthew R. McClure/Shutterstock

Respiratory and Circulatory System Interactions

Most animals need oxygen to live. Animal cells use oxygen to release energy from food. The *respiratory system* takes in oxygen and releases carbon dioxide. Depending on the animal, oxygen enters the body through the skin, lungs, gills, or other specialized organs. The oxygen can be delivered directly to the tissues and cells of the body, or it can be sent to the circulatory system. The *circulatory system* carries oxygen, water, and nutrients to all the cells of the body. In some animals, such as mammals, the circulatory system includes two subsystems: the cardiovascular system and the lymphatic system. The cardiovascular system includes the heart and blood vessels. The heart acts as a pump to move blood through the body's blood vessels. The lymphatic system transports fluid that helps the body fight infection.

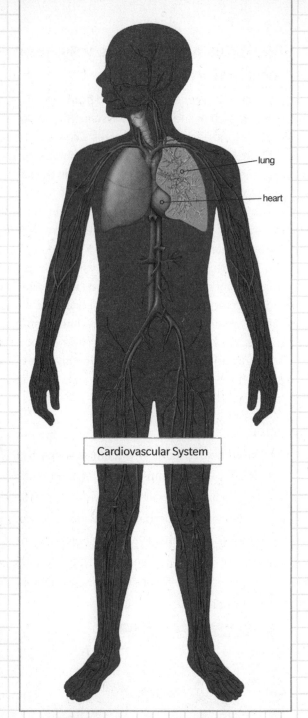

lung

heart

Cardiovascular System

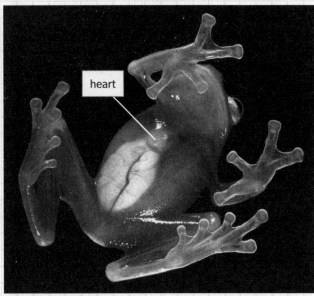

Frogs have a circulatory system and a respiratory system but can also absorb oxygen through their skin.

heart

4. A layer of water just under a frog's skin captures oxygen from air or water and delivers it to blood vessels at the skin's surface. How might this function relate to the fact that frogs are very sensitive to environmental pollution?

Skeletal and Muscular System Interactions

All animals are able to move at some point in their life cycle. The *muscular system* is a body system that provides internal and external movement for an animal. Most animals use muscles for movement, but some animals use other body structures, such as hair-like cilia.

Muscles attached to the skeleton produce movement. An animal skeleton can be made of bones or other hard, nonbony structures, such as spines or crystals. A skeleton can be external, like the exoskeleton of insects. An internal skeletal system, or endoskeleton, is a framework that provides support for the body.

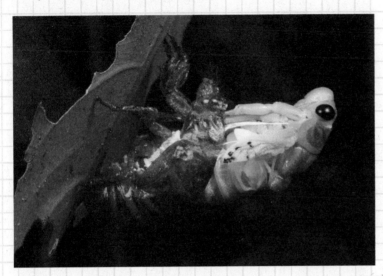

This cicada is *molting*, or shedding its exoskeleton.

5. The exoskeleton of an insect provides a stiff, protective armor. What might be some disadvantages of an exoskeleton?

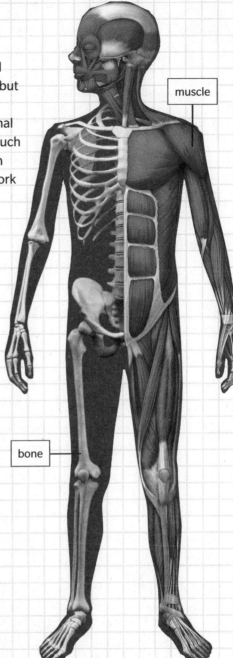

muscle

bone

Skeletal and Muscular Systems

Information Processing

All animals must be able to detect and react to conditions in their environments. The *nervous system* collects and processes information. The nervous system in most animals is a network of branching nerves that communicate messages between the brain and other parts of the body. In some animals, the brain is simply a cluster of nerve cells, while in others, it is complex and made up of many structures that work together.

Animals use a variety of structures to gather information from the environment. Eyes and ears are familiar organs, but animals also use hairs, skin, and antennae to collect information. Butterflies taste with their feet, and snakes smell with their tongues!

Measure System Response to Exercise

You will perform an exercise and measure the responses of your respiratory and cardiovascular systems.

When you exercise, your body systems work together to respond to changing needs for oxygen in your cells. Animals need more oxygen when they chase prey, run from predators, and travel long distances.

MATERIALS
- chair or other space to rest
- small space for exercising (for example, running in place)
- stopwatch

Procedure

STEP 1 Make a plan for how you will measure your breathing rate and pulse before you exercise. Decide how long you will rest before collecting the data.

STEP 2 Measure your before-exercise breathing rate and pulse. Record the data in the table below.

STEP 3 Make a plan for how you will measure your breathing rate and pulse after you exercise. Think about what type of exercise you will do and for how long.

STEP 4 Follow your plan to exercise. Measure your after-exercise breathing rate and pulse. Record the data for 3 trials in the table below.

STEP 5 Repeat the procedure two more times.

	Before Exercise		After Exercise	
	breathing rate	pulse	breathing rate	pulse
Trial 1				
Trial 2				
Trial 3				
Average				

Analysis and Conclusions

STEP 6 **Do the Math** For each column in your table, calculate the average of the three trials. Are the values recorded for each trial the same?

STEP 7 How did the change in pulse compare to the change in breathing rate? Did one change more than the other?

STEP 8 Look at the diagram that shows the connection between the circulatory and the respiratory systems. Use the diagram and your data to explain why pulse and breathing rates change when you exercise, and how the two systems are working together.

This diagram shows the path that blood takes through the human heart and lungs. Blood is pumped from the right side of the heart to the lungs. From the lungs, it returns to the left side of the heart. The blood is then pumped from the left side of the heart to the body. It flows to the tiny capillaries around every part of the body before returning to the right side of the heart.

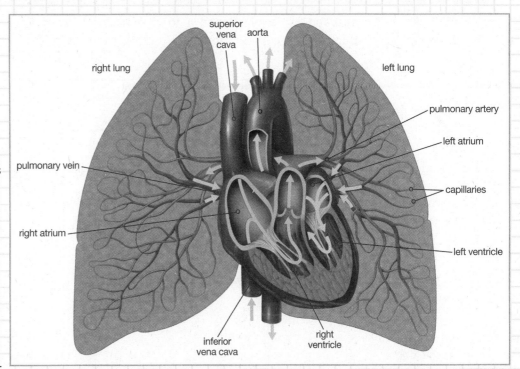

Design a Video Game Character

6. **Draw** Using drawing materials or digital tools, plan and draw a video game character based on an animal. The animal can have any features or functions you choose. Label the features and functions of your character.

Describing Information Processing in Animals

Think about what your body is doing right now. What can you see, feel, smell, and hear? Without even thinking about it, you are constantly receiving and processing information. Information processing causes you to respond to your environment, regulate the internal processes of your body, and learn and form memories from your experiences. The nervous system collects and processes information.

Animal Responses to Changes in Temperature

7. Think of some behaviors an animal might perform to warm up or cool down. Record the behaviors to complete the feedback diagram.

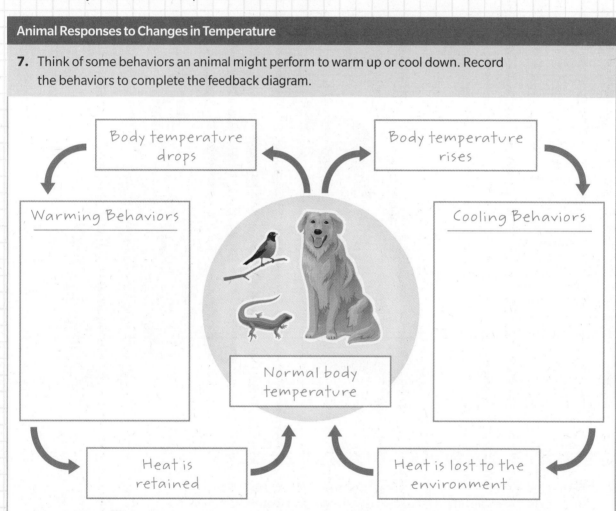

Homeostasis

In order to survive, an animal might need to respond to danger, the need for food and water, or changes in temperature. These responses help an animal maintain homeostasis. When internal and external environments change, **homeostasis** is the process by which the inside of the body maintains stable conditions. Homeostasis is controlled through feedback. Feedback is a cycle of events in which information from one step controls or affects a previous step. Feedback can be positive or negative. Negative feedback occurs when the body senses a change in its internal environment and activates processes that will slow or prevent the change. Positive feedback occurs when the body activates processes that increase or reinforce the change.

8. A dog responds to the stimulus of feeling hot by panting. When the dog cools down, the dog will stop panting. This way of controlling body temperature is an example of ~~negative/positive~~ feedback.

To help cool off, this dog is panting. Water evaporates from the dog's mouth, resulting in heat loss.

Sensing and Transmitting Information

Specialized cells in an animal's nervous system are called sensory receptors. **Sensory receptors** help an animal gather information about its environment. Sensory receptors are especially plentiful in sensory organs—the skin, ears, nose, mouth, and eyes—but they also occur in other parts of the body. Different types of sensory receptors respond to different environmental messages, such as light, heat, or pressure. This type of environmental message is called a *stimulus*. For example, a sensory receptor could detect pressure from a butterfly landing on your finger. When a sensory receptor detects a stimulus, it sends the information to the brain in the form of electrical energy. The information travels through specialized cells called *neurons*.

One group of neurons carries information from sensory receptors to the brain. Another group of neurons carries information from the brain to various parts of the body, telling them how to respond.

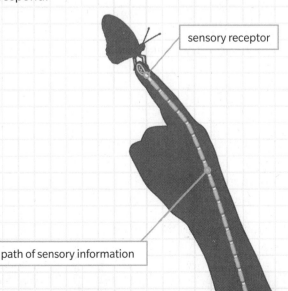

sensory receptor

neurons

path of sensory information

9. Read the descriptions about each animal below. Which stimulus might each of these animals be responding to? Use the terms in the Word Bank.

word bank	
• light	• odor
• motion	• sound

This male silkworm moth can detect very small concentrations of chemicals given off by a female.

Chameleons use highly coordinated eye movements to target their prey.

This spider is wrapping up prey that got caught in its web.

This serval hunts rodents that are scurrying through the grass.

Types of Sensory Receptors

Sensory receptors can be organized by the kind of stimuli they detect and respond to. *Mechanical receptors* detect pressure, movement, and tension. For example, fish have a specialized sense organ that detects vibrations in the water, helping them to navigate and hunt. Mechanical receptors also detect the motion of sound waves, allowing animals to hear.

Chemical receptors detect chemical signals, such as odors and tastes. Some animals have chemical receptors in their nose and mouth, but others have chemical receptors on their antennae or limbs.

Electromagnetic receptors detect electromagnetic radiation, such as light. Different kinds of animals have different electromagnetic receptors, so each kind of animal can see specific parts of the electromagnetic spectrum. Your eyes detect visible light, but some other animals can detect infrared radiation or ultraviolet light.

10. Discuss With a partner, discuss the types of receptors being used by the animals in the table.

Processing Sensory Information

Most animals have a brain that organizes and processes information from sensory receptors. Animal brains can be just a cluster of neurons, or they can be made up of many structures that work together. Different animals process information at different rates. For example, quick moving insects and small birds process visual information more rapidly than leatherback turtles do. Insects and birds need to respond quickly to catch prey or avoid being eaten by predators. Leatherback turtles move slowly and feed on slow-moving jellyfish, so fast visual processing does not provide a survival advantage.

Major Areas of the Human Cerebral Cortex

The illustration and the magnetic resonance image (MRI) both show the cerebral cortex of the human brain.

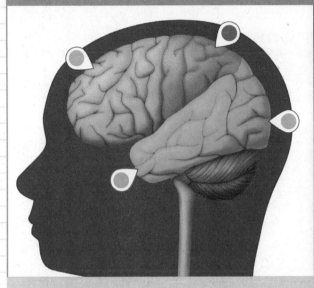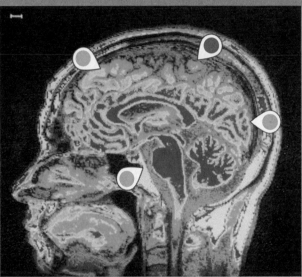

Frontal lobe
The frontal lobe is the "boss." It coordinates planning, organization, behaviors, and emotions.

Temporal lobe
The temporal lobe is associated with hearing, language, and olfactory senses.

Parietal lobe
The parietal lobe processes sensory information related to taste, temperature, and touch.

Occipital lobe
The occipital lobe is involved in the reception of visual stimuli.

11. You are walking down a busy street. The smell of freshly baked bread is coming from a bakery up ahead. You move to your right as a bike zooms past you. Suddenly, you hear a loud car horn directly behind you. Make a list of the information your brain is receiving in this scenario. Identify the areas of the brain that are involved in processing the different stimuli.

EVIDENCE NOTEBOOK

12. What types of stimuli is the fly responding to when you try to catch it? Which body systems might be involved in the response? Record your evidence.

Language SmArts
Explain Sensory Receptor Patterns

Not all parts of your body are as sensitive to touch as others. Your fingers, for example, have many sensory receptors, so they are very sensitive to touch. Other body parts—your back and your calf, for example—have fewer sensory receptors and are much less sensitive to touch.

Fingers are very sensitive to touch because they have so many mechanical receptors, as well as other types of sensory receptors.

13. Why do you think the parts of the body have different sensitivities? Write an argument to support your explanation.

_____
_____
_____
_____
_____
_____
_____
_____
_____
_____
_____

© Houghton Mifflin Harcourt Publishing Company • Image Credits: ©Herbie Springer/ Alamy Images

Analyzing Animal Responses to Information

When the brain receives sensory messages, it determines what to do with the information. Sensory inputs can result in an immediate response, and they can also be stored in the brain for use in the future. For example, an animal might perform the immediate behavior of spitting out a bad-tasting prey. The animal might also store that information as memory and avoid the prey when they meet again.

14. Look at the lion and the porcupines. What immediate behaviors might each animal perform? What might be stored as memory for each animal? Record your answers.

	behavior	memory
lion		
porcupines		

Behavior

The set of actions taken by an organism in response to stimuli is called **behavior**. Animals perform behaviors to survive. Some animal behaviors do not require learning or experience. For example, newborn whales know how to swim as soon as they are born. Behaviors that do not require learning or experience are called *innate* behaviors. Animals are born knowing these behaviors, but they are triggered by things that happen in the animal's environment.

Other behaviors develop through memories and experience, and from observing the actions of other animals. These behaviors that depend on memory are *learned* behaviors. For example, some birds learn their songs by listening to other individuals. Young animals can learn to hunt and even use tools by watching adults.

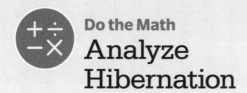

Do the Math

Analyze Hibernation

Hibernation is a behavior that allows animals to survive in their habitats during the winter months when food may be scarce. Animals that hibernate store body fat when food is plentiful. When food becomes scarce, they enter a period of inactivity, surviving off of their stored body fat. The graph below shows how two variables—weight gain and month of the year—relate to each other.

The hazel dormouse is a tiny rodent that hibernates for about half the year, from fall to spring.

15. The independent variable is the month of the year. The dependent variable is the average weight of the dormice. How are the two variables related to each other?

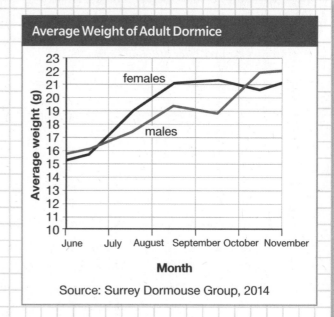

Average Weight of Adult Dormice

Source: Surrey Dormouse Group, 2014

16. During which time period do both the males and females gain weight most rapidly?

17. Write a short summary that explains the relationship between weight and hibernation.

Memory

Information can be stored in the brain as **memory**. Information that gets stored as memory can be an event, such as an encounter with predator or prey. Animals can also remember information related to sensory stimuli. Odor memory can help animals identify their infants or other family members. Visual memory can help them remember locations of food sources or migration routes. Memory allows an animal to respond to its environment more efficiently. For example, an animal that can remember the location of a food source will spend less time searching for food and more time eating!

Hands-On Lab
Measure Reaction Time

You will measure your reaction time in response to a falling object and compare your data with other groups.

Behaviors are the result of systems working together. To catch an object, your brain sends a message to the muscles in your arm. The time it takes for the message to travel from your brain to your arm is called your reaction time.

MATERIALS
• chair
• meterstick

Procedure and Analysis

STEP 1 One person should sit in a chair with one arm in a "handshake" position. The other person should stand facing the person in the chair, holding the meterstick vertically, so that the lower end is between the sitting person's thumb and forefinger. Observe where on the meterstick's scale the sitting person's thumb and forefinger are. Record the data in the table.

STEP 2 Make sure the sitting student has the thumb and forefinger far enough apart for the meterstick to fall through. The person holding the meterstick should drop it without warning. The person sitting should catch the meterstick as quickly as possible. Record the location of the sitting person's thumb and forefinger on the meterstick's scale after catching the meterstick.

STEP 3 Determine the distance the meterstick fell and record the data in the table.

STEP 4 Repeat Steps 1–3 two more times. Calculate the average distance the meterstick fell in the three trials.

	Finger position before drop (cm)	Finger position when caught (cm)	Distance meterstick fell (cm)
Trial 1			
Trial 2			
Trial 3			

Average distance meterstick fell: _____

STEP 5 Describe the flow of information from sensory receptors to behavioral response. Make note of all the body systems that are involved in the response you tested in this activity.

STEP 6 Compare your group's data with the data of another group. How did the data compare? What factors might explain any differences in reaction times?

STEP 7 **Discuss** In the activity, your reaction time probably got faster each time you caught the meterstick. With a partner, discuss how memory and experience contribute to a faster reaction time.

EVIDENCE NOTEBOOK

18. Look back at the photo of the fly. Does the fly have a fast reaction to your hand or a slow reaction? What effect might memory and experience have on the fly's reaction time in the long-term? Record your evidence.

Engineer It

Evaluate Biomimetics

Animals are often capable of sensing different information than humans. *Biomimicry,* or *biomimetics,* uses design solutions found in nature to solve human design problems. For example, brittle stars are covered in lenses that help them avoid predators. These lenses transmit light more perfectly than any human-made lens. Engineers designed improved lenses based on the brittle star lens structure that are soft, providing better fine-tuning and complexity than conventional hard lenses.

19. Why is it advantageous for engineers to look to animals for engineering design solutions?

_____

_____

_____

20. Bats detect objects using sound waves. The bat emits a sound from its mouth or nose. The sound wave hits an object and the echo returns to the bat's ear, which the bat uses to locate the object. Describe how this ability could be applied to the design of a cane used by visually-challenged people to navigate through their environments.

_____

_____

_____

_____

Continue Your Exploration

Name: _____   Date: _____

Check out the path below or go online to choose one of the other paths shown.

| Migration | • **Sensory Organ Adaptations**
• **Hands-On Labs** ✋
• **Propose Your Own Path** | *Go online to choose one of these other paths.* |

Animals travel long distances in response to seasonal weather changes and change in the availability of food. This type of travel is called *migration*. Migration is a seasonal movement from one place to another. Many birds, mammals, reptiles, fish, and even insects migrate. Animals make long journeys to escape harsh weather conditions, to find more abundant food, or to find more suitable locations for reproduction.

Unlike humans, animals do not have maps or instruments to navigate long distances. Animals might use the position of the sun or Earth's magnetic field to navigate. They can also use odor, sound waves, or the sight of familiar landmarks.

Monarch butterflies travel from the United States to Mexico to avoid the cold winter temperatures.

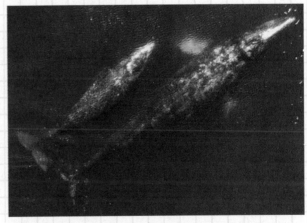

This gray whale and her calf are migrating north from California to summer feeding grounds in the Arctic.

1. If migration is thought of in terms of cause and effect, migration can be considered the effect. What is the cause of the monarch migration? What is the cause of the gray whale migration?

Continue Your Exploration

2. Scientists are not certain why the little Arctic tern makes the migration journey of 70,000 km round trip each year. Which statement below do you think is the most likely explanation?

    A. The Arctic terns are following patterns of food availability and favorable wind conditions from pole to pole.

    B. The Arctic terns are being carried from pole to pole by wind currents.

    C. The Arctic terns are traveling from pole to pole to find mates.

The Arctic tern makes the longest known annual migration—from the South Pole to the North Pole and back again.

3. Odor, or *olfactory*, memory plays a role in the migration of salmon, as well as some other animals. What type of sensory receptors do you think the salmon are using to navigate their migration path? Explain your answer.

Salmon hatch in fresh water and then migrate to the ocean. When salmon are ready to reproduce, they migrate back to the freshwater areas where they were hatched.

4. **Collaborate** Research a migration pattern of one of the animals from the previous page or another animal of your choice. Describe whether the cause of the migration is well-established, or if scientists have different opinions. Explain the possible role of memories in the behavior. Collaborate to make a visual summary or map of the pattern of migration.

Can You Explain It?

Name: _____ **Date:** _____

Why is it so difficult to catch a fly?

EVIDENCE NOTEBOOK

Refer to the notes in your Evidence Notebook to help you construct an explanation for why it is so difficult to catch a fly.

1. State your claim. Make sure your claim fully explains how the fly's body system works to respond to your grasp.

2. Summarize the evidence you have gathered to support your claim and explain your reasoning.

Checkpoints

Answer the following questions to check your understanding of the lesson.

Use the image to answer Questions 3–4.

3. The muscular / excretory system is interacting with the digestive / skeletal system to move the racer's arms.

4. Which body systems will interact to provide the energy the racer needs to keep pushing the wheels of the chair?

   A. digestive/excretory

   B. circulatory/respiratory

   C. muscular/skeletal

   D. digestive/circulatory

Use the image to answer Questions 5–6.

5. A scallop has as many as 100 bright blue eyes along the edges of its valves. What is the best explanation for having so many eyes?

   A. The scallop is able to detect the best time to reproduce.

   B. The scallop is able to detect predators from many directions.

   C. The scallop is able to detect a mate while swimming.

   D. The scallop is able to detect changes in water conditions.

6. Scallops use their shell valves to feed and move. A scallop opens its valves when it sees a food particle / predator nearby. It moves by clapping its valves together when it sees a food particle / predator nearby.

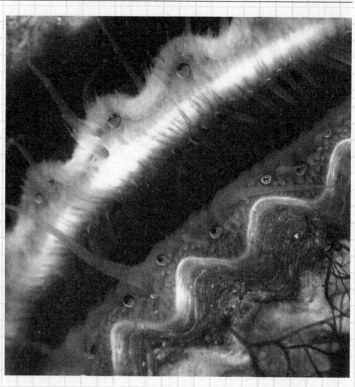

Interactive Review

Complete this section to review the main concepts of the lesson.

Animals are living systems made up of interacting subsystems that perform functions.

A. Describe the interaction of two body systems that perform a function needed by an animal to survive.

Animals gather and process information from their environment.

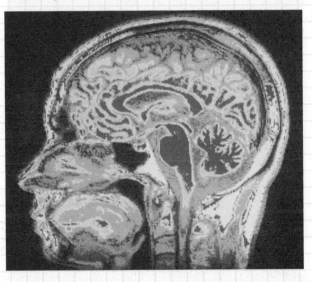

B. Draw a concept map or flow chart to show the path of an environmental stimulus to the brain.

Animals respond to stimuli by performing behaviors.

C. What is the relationship between memory and behavior?

Choose one of the activities to explore how this unit connects to other topics.

☐ People in Science

Garfield Kwan, Marine Biologist Garfield Kwan grew up in Hong Kong and Los Angeles. He studies marine biology at University of California in San Diego and is interested in how fish will respond to increased carbon dioxide levels in the ocean. Garfield knows that scientific concepts are often complex and that adding illustrations can make science easier to understand. He founded a company that creates infographics – a combination of illustrations and text – as a way to communicate complex scientific concepts in an interesting way. Research a natural system and create an infographic to explain the relationships among its components. Present your infographic to the class.

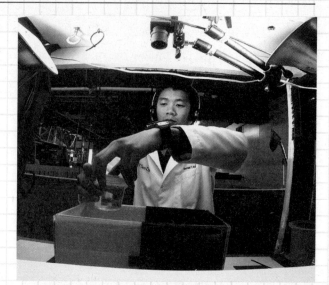

Garfield Kwan at work in the laboratory.

☐ Physical Science Connection

Scanning and Transmission Electron Microscopes In order to examine the smallest parts of cells in detail, scientists can use a scanning electron microscope or a transmission electron microscope. These types of microscopes use beams of electrons, rather than light. Using library or Internet resources, research how scanning electron microscopes (SEMs) and transmission electron microscopes (TEMs) work. Investigate the advantages and disadvantages of both types of microscope. Compare what is visible in a cell with a light microscope versus what is visible in a cell with a SEM or TEM. Create a multimedia presentation with your findings to share with the class.

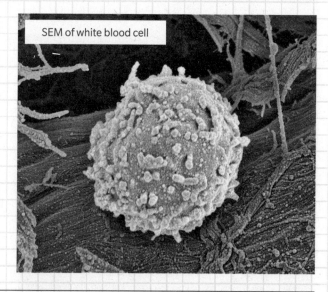

SEM of white blood cell

☐ Health Connection

Medical Research Neurological diseases affect components of the nervous system, including the brain, spinal cord, and neurons. Advances in gene mapping, stem cell therapy, and imaging technologies have improved understanding, diagnosis, and treatment of these diseases. Research a neurological disease, such as Alzheimer's disease or amyotrophic lateral sclerosis (ALS). Identify the causes and symptoms of the disease, and how current technologies are helping medical researchers diagnose and treat the disease. Write a magazine article to present your research.

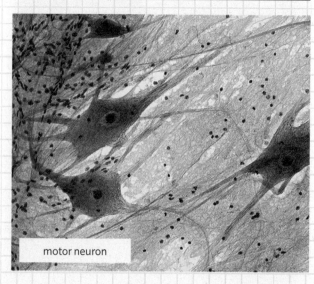

motor neuron

Name: _____ **Date:** _____

Use the diagram of the snake to answer Questions 1–3.

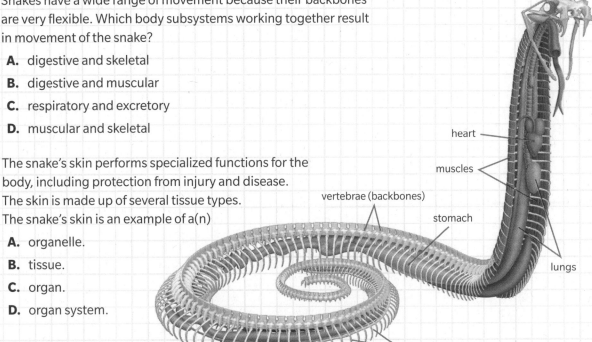

1. Snakes have a wide range of movement because their backbones are very flexible. Which body subsystems working together result in movement of the snake?

    A. digestive and skeletal

    B. digestive and muscular

    C. respiratory and excretory

    D. muscular and skeletal

2. The snake's skin performs specialized functions for the body, including protection from injury and disease. The skin is made up of several tissue types. The snake's skin is an example of a(n)

    A. organelle.

    B. tissue.

    C. organ.

    D. organ system.

3. The snake's skeletal system provides the function of transport / support, just as the root / shoot system does for a plant.

Use the photo to answer Questions 4–5.

4. Which Earth subsystem is not represented in the photo?

    A. geosphere

    B. hydrosphere

    C. cryosphere

    D. atmosphere

5. The Golden Gate Bridge is part of the geosphere / anthroposphere. It connects two sections of land previously separated by the biosphere / hydrosphere. The movement of animals across the bridge has resulted in changes in populations in the biosphere / atmosphere on each side of the bridge.

6. For each of the body functions listed, describe the function in terms of cause and effect. Identify the plant and/or animal systems involved, and describe any related patterns between plant and animal bodies.

Body Functions	Systems	Cause-and-Effect Relationships	Patterns in Plant and Animal Bodies
Moving water and nutrients throughout body			
Getting energy from food			
Providing support for the body			
Regulating oxygen and carbon dioxide			
Responding to the environment			

Name: _____   Date: _____

Use the illustration of the frog to answer Questions 7–11.

7. Identify the environmental stimulus that the frog is perceiving.

8. Explain how both electromagnetic receptors and mechanical receptors might be involved in sensing this stimulus.

9. Describe how sensory receptors transmit information about the stimulus to the frog's brain.

10. Describe the frog's possible responses to the information the sensory receptors have transmitted to the brain. Include a description of how the brain will cause the frog's body to act.

11. A frog's response to prey is innate. Explain how the response time might change over the life of the frog.

Use the illustration to answer Questions 12–15.

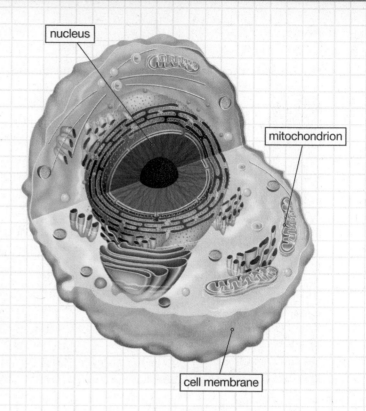

nucleus

mitochondrion

cell membrane

12. Is the cell shown in the illustration a bacterial, plant, or animal cell? Support your claim with evidence from the illustration.

13. Describe the cell as a system of interacting parts. Include the parts of the system in your description.

14. Describe how cell system function might be affected if one or more components were not functional.

15. What are some advantages of this cell illustration ? What are some limitations of this cell illustration?

Name: _____ Date: _____

How can dehydration be prevented?

Your school district wants to find the best ways to keep student athletes from becoming dehydrated during afterschool practices. You have been asked to help school officials, coaches, and parent volunteers devise a plan for keeping student athletes hydrated. Study the diagram below, which shows some of the body systems involved in maintaining water balance in the body.

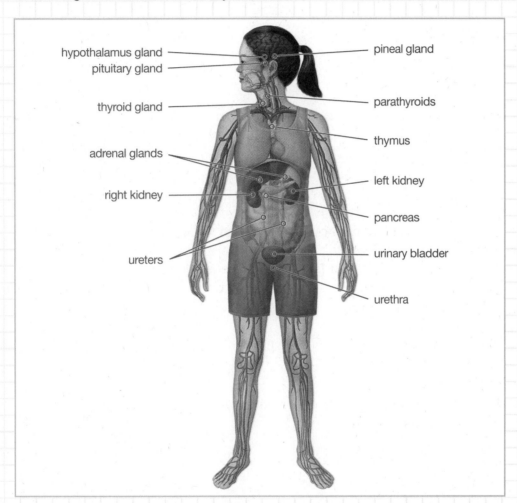

The steps below will help guide your research and develop your recommendation.

Engineer It

1. **Define the Problem** Investigate the importance of water in human body systems. Define the problem you are trying to solve.

Engineer It

2. **Conduct Research** Investigate the body systems involved in maintaining water balance in the body. Research the causes and symptoms of dehydration in the human body.

3. **Analyze a System Response** Choose one of the body systems that shows symptoms of dehydration, and analyze the cause and effect of the system's response to dehydration.

4. **Propose a Solution** Brainstorm solutions to the problem of how to keep student athletes hydrated during practices. Make a recommendation based on your research. Explain how the solution would work with the body system you identified to bring the body back to homeostasis after dehydration.

5. **Communicate Your Findings** Create a presentation that summarizes your findings and explains your solution.

 **Self-Check**

	I defined the problem of preventing dehydration in student athletes and investigated the importance of water to human body systems.
	I investigated the body systems involved in maintaining water balance in the body and researched causes and symptoms of dehydration.
	I analyzed the causes and effects of a body system's response to dehydration.
	I recommended a solution to the problem of preventing dehydration in student athletes and explained how the solution would work with the body system to bring the body back to homeostasis.
	I clearly communicated my findings and explained my solution.

Go online to access the **Interactive Glossary**. You can use this online tool to look up definitions for all the vocabulary terms in this book.

Pronunciation Key

Sound	Symbol	Example	Respelling	Sound	Symbol	Example	Respelling
ă	a	pat	PAT	ŏ	ah	bottle	BAHT'l
ā	ay	pay	PAY	ō	oh	toe	TOH
âr	air	care	KAIR	ô	aw	caught	KAWT
ä	ah	father	FAH•ther	ôr	ohr	roar	ROHR
är	ar	argue	AR•gyoo	oi	oy	noisy	NOYZ•ee
ch	ch	chase	CHAYS	ōō	u	book	BUK
ĕ	e	pet	PET	ōō	oo	boot	BOOT
ĕ (at end of a syllable)	eh	settee lessee	seh•TEE leh•SEE	ou	ow	pound	POWND
ĕr	ehr	merry	MEHR•ee	s	s	center	SEN•ter
ē	ee	beach	BEECH	sh	sh	cache	CASH
g	g	gas	GAS	ŭ	uh	flood	FLUHD
ĭ	i	pit	PIT	ûr	er	bird	BERD
ĭ (at end of a syllable)	ih	guitar	gih•TAR	z	z	xylophone	ZY•luh•fohn
ī	y eye (only for a complete syllable)	pie island	PY EYE•luhnd	z	z	bags	BAGZ
îr	ir	hear	HIR	zh	zh	decision	dih•SIZH•uhn
j	j	germ	JERM	ə	uh	around broken focus	uh•ROWND BROH•kuhn FOH•kuhs
k	k	kick	KIK	ər	er	winner	WIN•er
ng	ng	thing	THING	th	th	thin they	THIN THAY
ngk	ngk	bank	BANGK	w	w	one	WUHN
				wh	hw	whether	HWETH•er

Index

Page numbers for key terms are in **boldface** type.
Page numbers in *italic* type indicate illustrative material, such as photographs, graphs, charts, and maps.

A

acidic water, 539, *539*
acid rain, 496
Act, 210, 274, 343
adaptation, 391
   in chaparral ecosystem, 536, *536*
   environment affecting, *393*, 394
   of organism, 391, 534–537
   types of, 392
adaptive technologies, 18
adenine, 411
adrenal gland, 171, *171*
advantages, 65
aerodynamics, 8, *8*
aerosols, 527
African cichlid fish, 400, *400*
African elephants, 532
aggregating anemone, 461, *461*
agricultural areas, 387
agriculture
   geosphere affected by, 495
   modeling runoff, 100
   water needs of, 493
air
   atmosphere as, 270
   circulation of, 275–278, 279–282
   currents, 98
   mass of, 319–320, *319*, 326, 331, 359
   as matter, 279
   movement of, 268–287
   particles of, 294, *312*, 314
   quality of, 556–558
air mass, 319
air pollution, 495
air pressure
   element of weather, 314
   formation of, 271–272
   identifying weather associated with, 316–318
   map of, 316
   prevailing wind and, *324*
   system of, 317–318, *317*

   temperature differences causing, 275
   on weather map, *318*
   wind formation caused by, 315
air temperature
   air pressure changes caused by, 275
   clouds effect on, 313
   cricket chirps estimating, 339, *339*
   differences in cause wind, 272
   differences of changing air density, 272
   affecting precipitation, 313
   pressure affected by, 316, *316*
   thermal energy of, 208
   during water changing states, 240, *240*
air travel, 581–582
Akashi Kaikyō Bridge, 62, *62*
Alaska, 384, *384*
Alaskan Inuit Culture, 372, *372*
albedo, 356–357
algae, 90, 101, 425, 489, *489*, 500
allele, 404, 408, *408*
Alpine butterfly, 393, *393*
Alpine wildflower, 350, *350*
alternative energy, 191, 219, *230*, 563
altitude, 360, 361, *361*, 371, 384, *385*, 399
Alturas, California, 366, *366*
alumina refining, 564, *564*
aluminum, 205, 223, 564, *564*
Alvin, 305, *305*
Amazon, 269, *269*, 285, *285*
ambient temperature, 220
American pika, 393, *393*
amoebas, 419
amphibian, 423, *423*, 458, *458*
analysis
   of air mass interaction, 320
   of animal body systems, 146–151
   of board game, 471
   of cells, 113, 115–118, 120–121
   of climate model, 363
   of clouds and rain formation, 243
   of cod population, 502

   of cost-benefit, 45, 65
   of data, 52, 54, 56, 65, 378
   of drought tolerance of plants, 389–390
   of energy transfer, 185
   of factors determining climate, 384–386
   of female mate choice, 465
   of flower parts, 443
   of formation of wind, 271–272
   of greenhouse effect, 512
   of heat, 208–210
   of hibernation, 158
   of honeybee colony loss, 445
   of impact of technology on society, 20
   of insulated container, 229–230
   in investigations, 20
   of model car, 71–72
   of models, 88
   of monarch migration, 540–541
   of pollution, 494
   of processes, 248
   of reaction time, 159
   of relationships between structure and function, 20
   of resource quality data, 557
   of resource use data, 555–556
   of risk-benefit analysis, 49
   of shipping costs, *337*
   of solar water heater, *220*
   of solid waste reduction, 569–570
   of system responses to exercise, 150
   of technological influences, *13*
   of thermal energy loss, 201
   of thermal energy transfer, 222
   of tissue, 94
   of water density, 295
   of water on Earth, 238–240
   of weather forecast map, 343, *343*, 344, *344*
   of wind, 274
Analyze Geothermal Heat Pumps, 230

E

ear, 149, 153

Earth

absorbing and reflecting sunlight, 354, *354*, 511, *511*

albedo, 356–357

changes in orbit of, 515, 516

climates of, 350–366, *362*, *364–365*, 371, 384, *384*

diversity of living things on, 418

satellites orbiting, 85

surface changes of, 516

surface temperature changes, 520, *520*

Earth Science Connection

Climate and Reproduction, 478

Earth's rotation

causing winds and air currents, 98

Coriolis effect, 276, *276*

effect on gyres patterns, 292–293, *293*

effect on pressure systems, 317, *317*

jet streams caused by, 283, *283*

matter in atmosphere effected by, 275

Earth System

air circulation relating to, 279–282

air movement patterns in atmosphere of, 268–287

air pressure in, 314, *314*

analyzing water on, 238–240

carbon cycle on, *304*

climate system, 511–513

cycling of matter in, 303

energy flow in, 174

ice on surface of, 248, *248*

interaction in, 89, 310–327, 511

modeling of, 97–102

movement of water on, 245–246, 288–305

states of water on, 239–240

subsystems of, 97–102, *97*, 270, 300

Eastern gray squirrel, 458, *458*

***E. coli* bacteria,** 93, *93*

economy, 100

ecosystem, 534

biodiversity of, 535, 551

climate change disrupting, 538

dam system disrupting, 247

habitat degradation, 542

health of, 534–535

importance of, 544

levels of, 534, *534*

roads affecting, 16

Eco-Task Force, 483

Edison, Thomas, 44, 57

egg

of aggregating anemone, 461, *461*

of birds, 459, *459*, 464

of dragonflies, 458

of fish, 420, *420*, 459, *459*, 553, *553*

of flowering plants, 441

of octopus, 464

parents protecting, 464

of seedless plants, 437, *437*

of seed plants, 438

elastic potential energy, 181

electrical current, 182

electrical energy

defined, 181–182

reducing use of, 570, *570*

sensory response, 153

from steam turbines, 567, *567*

transformation of, 190, *190*

electrical engineer, 73–74

electric circuits in computers, 14

electromagnetic energy, 181, 190, *190*, 219

electromagnetic receptor, 154

electron microscope, 111

elephant, 419, 456, *456*

elephant seal, 462

elevation, 360, 361, *361*, 371, 385, *385*

elk, 463, *463*, 535

Ellesmere Island, Canada, 364, *364*

El Niño, 518, *518*, 539

embryo

of fish, 118, *118*

of mollusk, 458

of plants, 438, 446

Emperor penguin, 383, 397, *397*

endoplasmic reticulum, 116, *116*, 117, *117*

endoskeleton, 149

endosymbiosis, 123

energy

causing changes, 178

clouds absorbing, 313

collision transferring, 186–187

convection transferring, 300–301

Earth balancing, 354, *354*, 511, *511*

in Earth systems, 97

flowing and causing change, 176–196

flow of in atmosphere, 281, 287

flow of in oceans, 303, 309

flow of in systems, 173–264

flow of water cycle, 251

forms of, 181–182

gravitational potential energy, 180–181

hydroelectric power station transforming, 176

identifying forms of, 178–183

kinetic, 178–179

law of conservation of energy, 180

loss in systems, 191–192

mechanical energy, 181–182

modeling transformation of, 189–192

moving through biosphere, 99

observing transfer of, 184–188

from photosynthesis, 90, 130

potential energy, 180–181

in radiometer, 218

stored, 180–181

from sun, 98, 303

surface wind and surface current transferring, 292

in systems, 90

thermal energy, 98, 189

transfers of within a system, 90, 178

in water cycle, 98

from wind, 39–40

energy conservationist, 231–232

energy drive, in water cycle, 236–257

energy efficient, 192

energy-efficient appliance, 563

energy-efficient home, 232, *232*

© Houghton Mifflin Harcourt Publishing Company

F

© Houghton Mifflin Harcourt Publishing Company

© Houghton Mifflin Harcourt Publishing Company

© Houghton Mifflin Harcourt Publishing Company